Pope Pius IV

## The Grounds of the Catholick Doctrine

Contained in the Profession of Faith. Eighth Edition

Pope Pius IV

**The Grounds of the Catholick Doctrine**
*Contained in the Profession of Faith. Eighth Edition*

ISBN/EAN: 9783337063634

Printed in Europe, USA, Canada, Australia, Japan

Cover: Foto ©Lupo / pixelio.de

More available books at **www.hansebooks.com**

# THE
# GROUNDS
OF THE

## Catholick Doctrine,

Contained in the

## Profeffion of FAITH,

PUBLISH'D BY

## Pope *PIUS* the Fourth,

BY WAY OF

## QUESTION and ANSWER.

---

The EIGHTH EDITION.

---

*Be ready always to give an Anfwer to every one that afketh you a Reafon of the Hope that is in you.* 1 Peter iii. 15.

---

*PRESTON:*
PRINTED BY W. STUART.

M DCC LXXV.

Whofoever will be faved : Before all Things
it is neceffary that he hold the Catholick
Faith. Which Faith except every one do
keep whole and undefiled : Without doubt
he fhall perifh everlaftingly. St. *Athanafius*'s
*Creed.*

## A

# PROFESSION

### OF

## CATHOLICK FAITH, &c.

*N. N.* with a firm Faith believe and profefs all and every one of thofe Things, which are contained in that Creed, which the Holy *Roman* Church maketh ufe of. To wit, I believe in one God, the *Father* Almighty, Maker of Heaven and Earth, of all Things vifible and invifible: And in one Lord *Jefus Chrift,* the only begotten *Son* of God, and born of the Father before all Ages; God of God; Light of Light; true God of the true God; begotten, not made; confubftantial to the Father, by whom all Things were made. Who for us Men, and for our Salvation, came down from Heaven, and was incarnate by the Holy Ghoft of the Virgin *Mary,* and was made Man. Was crucified alfo for us under *Pontius Pilate*; he fuffered and was buried: And the third Day he rofe again, according to the Scriptures: He afcended into Heaven; fits at the Right-hand of the Father, and is to come again with Glory to judge the Living and the Dead; of whofe Kingdom there fhall be no End. And in the *Holy Ghoft,* the Lord and Life-giver, who proceeds from the Father and the Son, who together with the Father and

the

the Son, is adored and glorified, who fpoke by the
Prophets. And [I believe] one, holy, Catholick,
and Apoftolick *Church*: I confefs one Baptifm for
the Remiffion of Sins: And I look for the Refurrection of the Dead, and the Life of the World to
come. *Amen.*

I moft ftedfaftly admit and embrace Apoftolical
and Ecclefiaftical *Traditions,* and all other Obfervances and Conftitutions of the fame Church.

I alfo admit the holy *Scriptures* according to that
Senfe which our holy Mother, the Church, has
held, and does hold, to which it belongs to *judge*
of the true Senfe and Interpretation of the Scriptures:
Neither will I ever take and interpret them otherwife than according to the unanimous Confent of the
Fathers.

I alfo profefs, that there are truly and properly
*Seven Sacraments* of the New Law, inftituted by
*Jefus Chrift,* our Lord, and neceffary for the Salvation of Mankind, tho' not all for every one: To
wit, *Baptifm, Confirmation, Eucharift, Penance, Extreme Unction, Order,* and *Matrimony:* And that
they confer Grace: And that of thefe, *Baptifm,
Confirmation,* and *Order,* cannot be reiterated without Sacrilege. I alfo receive and admit the received
and approved *Ceremonies* of the *Catholick* Church,
ufed in the folemn Adminiftration of all the afore-
faid Sacraments.

I embrace and receive all and every one of the
Things which have been defined and declared in the
holy Council of *Trent,* concerning *Original Sin* and
*Juftification.*

I profefs likewife, that in the *Mafs* there is offered to God a true, proper, and propitiatory Sacrifice for the Living and the Dead. And that *in the
moft holy Sacrament of the Eucharift, there is truly,
really, and fubftantially, the Body and Blood, together
with the Soul and Divinity of our Lord* Jefus Chrift:
    And

And that there is made a Converfion of the whole Subftance of the Bread into the Body, and of the whole Subftance of the Wine into the Blood; which Converfion the *Catholick* Church calls *Tranfubftantiation*. I alfo confefs, that under *either kind* alone *Chrift* is received whole and entire, and a true Sacrament.

I conftantly hold, that there is a *Purgatory*, and that the Souls therein detained are helped by the Suffrages of the Faithful.

Likewife, that the *Saints*, reigning together with *Chrift*, are to be honoured and invocated, and that they offer Prayers to God for us, and that their *Relicks* are to be had in Veneration.

I moft firmly affert, that the *Images* of *Chrift*, of the Mother of God, ever Virgin, and alfo of other Saints, ought to be had and retained, and that due Honour and Veneration is to be given them.

I alfo affirm, that the Power of *Indulgences* was left by *Chrift* in the Church, and that the Ufe of them is moft wholefome to *Chriftian* People.

I acknowledge the *Holy, Catholick, Apoftolick, Roman Church* for the Mother and Miftrefs of all Churches; and I promife true Obedience to the *Bifhop* of *Rome*, Succeffor to St. *Peter*, Prince of the Apoftles, and Vicar of *Jefus Chrift*.

I likewife undoubtedly receive and profefs all other Things delivered, defined, and declared by the facred Canons and General Councils, and particularly by the holy Council of *Trent*. And I condemn, reject, and anathematize all Things contrary thereto, and all Herefies which the Church has condemned, rejected, and anathematized.

I *N. N.* do at this prefent freely profefs, and fincerely hold this true Catholick Faith, without which no one can be faved: And I promife moft conftantly to retain and confefs the fame entire and unviolated, with God's Affiftance, to the End of my Life.

A 3

*The*

# The Grounds of the Catholick Doctrine, contained in the Profession of Faith of Pius IV.

## CHAP. I.

### Of the Church.

Q. *WHAT is your Profession as to the Article of the Church ?*

*A.* It is contained in thofe Words of the *Nicene* Creed, *I believe One Holy, Catholick, and Apoftolick Church.*

Q. *What do you gather from thefe Words ?*

*A.* 1. That *Jefus Chrift* has always a true Church upon Earth. 2. That this Church.is always *one* by the Union of all her Members in one *Faith* and Communion. 3. That fhe is always *pure* and *holy* in her Doctrine and Terms of Communion, and confequently always free from pernicious Errors. 4. That fhe is *Catholick,* that is, *Univerfal,* by being the Church of all Ages, and more or lefs of all Nations. 5. That this Church muft have in her a Succeffion from the *Apoftles,* and a lawful Miffion derived from them. 6. (Which follows from all the reft.) That this true Church of *Chrift* cannot be any of the *Proteftant* Sects, but muft be the ancient Church communicating with the Pope or Bifhop of *Rome.*

### Sect. 1. *That* Chrift *has always a true Church upon Earth.*

Q. *How do you prove that* Chrift *has always a true Church upon Earth ?*

*A.* From many plain Texts of Scripture, in which it is promifed or foretold that the Church or Kingdom

dom establish'd by *Christ* should stand till the End of the World. *Matthew* xvi. *v.* 18. *Thou art* Peter [i. e. a Rock] *and upon this Rock will I build my church, and the gates of hell shall not prevail against it.* Matthew xxviii. *v.* 19, 20. *Go ye therefore and teach all Nations, baptizing them,* &c. *teaching them to observe all Things whatsoever I have commanded you: And behold I am with you always even to the end of the world.* Pf. lxxii. *v.* 5, 7. *They shall fear thee as long as the fun and moon endure, throughout all generations---In his days,* [that is, after the coming of *Christ*] *shall the righteous flourish and abundance of peace, so long as the moon endureth.* Daniel ii. *v.* 44. *In the Days of these Kings shall the God of heaven set up a kingdom* [the Church or Kingdom of *Christ*] *which shall never be destroy'd-- and it shall stand for ever.*

Q. *What other Proof have you for the perpetual Continuance of the Church of* Christ?

A. The *Creed*, in which we profess to believe *the holy* Catholick *Church*. For the *Creed* and every Article thereof must be always true ; and therefore there must always be a holy *Catholick* Church.

Q. *Can you prove that* Christ's *Church upon Earth is always Visible?*

A. Yes, from many Texts of Scripture, as *Isaiah* ii. *v.* 1, 2, 3, &c. and *Micah* iv. *v.* 1, 2. where the Church of *Christ* is described as a *mountain upon the top of mountains*, expofed *to* the View *of all nations flowing unto it.* And *Daniel* ii. *v.* 35. *as a great mountain filling the whole Earth.* Matt. v. *v.* 14. *as a city set on a hill which cannot be hid.* Ifaiah lx. *v.* 11, 12. as a City whofe *gates shall be open continually ; and shall not be shut day nor night, that men may bring* thither *the forces of the* Gentiles, *and that their kings may be brought.* Upon the *walls* of which City God has *set watchmen.* Ifaiah lxii. *v.* 6. *which shall never hold their Peace day nor night.*

Sect,

SECT. 2. *That* Christ's *Church upon Earth in always* ONE.

*Q. How do you prove that* Christ's *Church upon Earth can be but One ?*

*A.* From many Texts of Scripture, *Song of* Solomon vi. *v.* 9, 10. *My dove, my undefiled is* BUT ONE,---*Fair as the moon, clear as the sun, terrible as an army with banners.* John x. *v.* 16. *Other sheep I have which are not of this fold (viz.* the *Gentiles,* who were then divided from the *Jews) them also I must bring, and they shall hear my voice, and there shall be* ONE FOLD AND ONE SHEPHERD. Ephef. iv. *v.* 4, 5. *There is* ONE *Body and* ONE *Spirit, as you are call'd in* ONE *Hope of your calling,* ONE *Lord,* ONE *Faith,* ONE *Baptism.* In fine, as we have seen already, the Church of *Christ* is a Kingdom which shall stand for ever ; and therefore must be always *One.* *For every kingdom divided against itself is brought to desolation, and every city or house divided against itself shall not stand.* Matt. xii. *v.* 25.

*Q. May not Persons be saved in any Religion?*

*A.* No certainly : St. *Paul* tells us, *Heb.* xi. *v.* 6. *That without Faith it is impossible to please God :* And St. *Peter* assures us, *Acts* iv. *v.* 12. *That there is no other name under heaven given to men by which we may be saved, but the Name of* Jesus : And *Christ* himself tells us, *Mark* xvi. *v.* 16. *He that believeth not, shall be damn'd.* So that it is manifest from the holy Scripture, that *true Faith* is necessary to Salvation. Now *true Faith,* in order to please God, and save our Souls, must be *entire* ; that is to say, must believe without Exception all such Articles as by God and his Church are proposed to be believed : And he that voluntarily and obstinately disbelieveth any one of these Articles, is no less void of *true* saving *Faith* than he that disbelieves them all : As St. *James* tells us, with regard to practical Duties,

chap.

chap. ii. *v.* 10. *Whosoever shall keep the whole law, yet offend in one point, he is guilty of all.* Hence St. *Paul, Gal.* v. *v.* 20. reckons *Heresies,* that is, false Religions, amongst those Works of the Flesh, of which he pronounces, *that they who do such things shall not inherit the kingdom of God :* And God himself, *Isaiah* lx. *v.* 12. tells his Church, *the nation and kingdom that will not serve thee, shall perish.*

Q. *Can any one be out of the Way of Salvation without the Guilt of mortal Sin ?*

*A.* No. But all such, as through Obstinacy, Negligence, or Indifference in Matters of Religion, will not hear the true Church and her Pastors, are guilty of mortal Sin. *Matt.* xviii. *v.* 17. *If he neglect to hear the church, let him be to thee as a heathen and a publican.* Luke x. *v.* 16. *He that heareth you* [the Pastors of the Church] *heareth me; and he that despiseth you, despiseth me ; and he that despiseth me, despiseth him that sent me.*

Q. *But what do you think of those whose* Conscience *persuades them they are in the true Church?*

*A.* If this Error of theirs proceed from *invincible Ignorance,* they may be excused from the Sin of Heresy; provided that in the sincere Dispositions of their Hearts they would gladly embrace the Truth, if they could find it out, in spite of all Opposition of Interest, Passion, &c. But if this *Error* of their Conscience be not *invincible,* but such as they might discover, if they were in earnest, in a Matter of so great a Consequence; their Conscience will not excuse them, no more than St. *Paul's,* whilst out of blind Zeal he persecuted the Church; or the mistaken Conscience of the *Jews,* when putting the Disciples of *Christ* to Death they thought they did a Service to God, *John* xvi. *v.* 2. *For there is a way that seemeth right unto Man ; but the end thereof are the ways of death.* Proverbs xvi. *v.* 25.

Q. *But does not the Scripture somewhere say,* That a Remnant of all *Religions* shall be saved ? *A.*

*A.* No: Tho' I have often heard fuch Words al-
ledged by *Proteſtants,* they are not any-where to be
found in Scripture, from the Beginning of *Geneſis* to
the End of *Revelation.* I ſuppoſe what has given
Occaſion to their Miſtake muſt have been the Words
of St. *Paul, Romans* ix. *v.* 27. where quoting *Iſaiah*
x. *v.* 22. he tells us, *Tho' the number of the children
of* Iſrael *be as the ſand of the ſea,* a remnant (that is,
a ſmall Part of them only) *ſhall be ſaved :* Which
Remnant the Apoſtle himſelf explains, *Rom.* xi. *v.* 5.
of ſuch of the *Jewiſh* Nation as at that Time by en-
tring into the Church were ſaved by God's Grace.
But what is this to a Salvation of a Remnant of all
Religions? A Doctrine ſo viſibly contradicting the
Scripture, that even the *Engliſh* Proteſtant Church
herſelf, in the 18th of her 39 Articles, has declared
them to be *accurſed* who preſume to maintain it.

SECT. 3. *That the Church of* Chriſt *is always*
Holy *in her Doctrine and Terms of Com-*
*munion, and always free from pernicious*
*Errors.*

Q. *How do you prove this ?*
*A.* 1ſt, Becauſe, as we have ſeen above from *Matt.*
xvi. *v.* 18. our Lord *Jeſus Chriſt,* who cannot tell
us a Lie, has promiſed that his *Church* ſhould be
*built upon a Rock,* Proof againſt all Floods and Storms,
like the Houſe of the wiſe Builder, of whom he
ſpeaks, *Matt.* vii. *v.* 25. and that *the Gates of Hell,*
that is, the Power of Darkneſs, ſhould never *prevail*
*againſt it.* Therefore the Church of *Chriſt* could
never ceaſe to be *Holy* in her Doctrine; could never
fall into Idolatry, Superſtition, or any heretical Errors whatſoever.

2dly, Becauſe *Chriſt,* who *is the way, the truth and*
*the life,* John xiv. *v.* 6. has promiſed, *Matt.* xxviii.
*v.* 19, 20. to the Paſtors and Teachers of his Church,
to

to *be with them always, even to the end of the world.*
Therefore they could never go aftray by pernicious
Errors : For how could they go out of the right
*Way* of *Truth* and *Life*, who are affured to have al-
ways in their Company, for their Guide, him who
is the *Way*, the *Truth*, and the *Life*.

3*dly*, Becaufe our Lord has promifed to the fame
Teachers, *John* xiv. *v.* 16, 17. *I will pray the Father,*
*and he fhall give you another Comforter, that he may*
*abide with you* FOR EVER, *even the* SPIRIT of
TRUTH. And *v.* 16, he affured them that this Spirit
of Truth *fhall teach them* ALL THINGS: And *c.* xvi.
*v.* 13, that he *fhall guide them* INTO ALL TRUTH.
How then could it be poffible that the whole Body
of thefe Paftors and Teachers of the Church, who,
by Virtue of thefe Promifes, were to be *for ever*
guided *into all Truth* by *the Spirit of Truth*, fhall at
any Time fall from the Truth by Errors in Faith?

4*thly*, Becaufe, *Ifaiah* lix. *v.* 20, 21. God has
made a folemn Covenant, that after the Coming of
our Redeemer, his *Spirit* and his *Words*, that is, the
whole Doctrine which this Redeemer was to teach,
fhall be for ever maintained by his Church through
all Generations. *The Redeemer fhall come to* Zion, &c.
*This is my Covenant with them, faith the Lord : My*
*Spirit which is upon thee, and my words which I have*
*put in thy mouth, fhall not depart out of thy mouth, nor*
*out of the mouth of thy feed, nor out of the mouth of*
*thy feed's feed, faith the Lord, from henceforth and for*
*ever.*

5*thly*, Becaufe the Church of *Chrift* is reprefented,
*Ifaiah* xxxv. *v.* 8. as a *high way, a way of holinefs,*
a Way fo plain and fo fecure, that even *fools fhould*
*not err therein.* How then could it ever be poffible
that the Church herfelf fhould err ?

6*thly*, Becaufe pernicious Errors in Faith and
Morals muft needs be fuch as to provoke God's
Indignation: Now God Almighty has promifed to
his

his Church, *Isaiah* liv. *v.* 9, 10. *As I have sworn that the waters of* Noah *should no more go over the earth, so have I sworn, that I would not be wrath with thee, nor rebuke thee: For the mountains shall depart, and the hills be removed: But my kindness shall not depart from thee, neither shall the covenant of my peace be removed, saith the Lord, that hath mercy on thee,* So that, as we are assured that there shall not be a second Flood; so we are that the Church of *Christ* shall never draw upon herself the Wrath of God by teaching Errors contrary to Faith.

In fine, the Church is called by St. *Paul,* 1 *Timothy* iii. *v.* 15. *The pillar and ground of the Truth.* Therefore she cannot uphold pernicious Errors. From all which it is manifest, that the Church of *Christ* is *infallible* in all Matters relating to Faith; so that she can neither add nor retrench from what *Christ* taught.

## SECT. 4. *That the Church of* Christ *is* Catholick *or* Universal.

*Q. What do you understand by this?*

*A.* Not only, that the Church of *Christ* shall always be known by the Name of *Catholick,* by which she is call'd in the Creed; but that she shall also be truly *Catholick* or *Universal,* by being the Church of all Ages, and of all Nations.

*Q. How do you prove that the true Church of* Christ *must be the Church of all Ages?*

*A.* Because the true Church of *Christ* must be that which had its Beginning from *Christ*; and, as he promised, was to continue to the End of the World. See *Sect.* 1, *and* 3.

*Q. How do you prove, that the true Church of* Christ *must be the Church of all Nations.*

*A.* From many Texts of Scripture, in which the true Church of *Christ* is always represented as a numerous

merous Congregation spread through the World. *Genesis* xxii. *v.* 18. *In thy feed shall all the Nations of the earth be blessed.* Psalm ii. *v.* 8. *Ask of me, and I shall give thee the heathen for thine inheritance; and the uttermost parts of the earth for thy possession.* Psal. xxii. *v.* 27. *All the ends of the world shall remember and turn unto the Lord, and all the kindreds of the nations shall worship before thee.* Isaiah xlix. *v.* 6. *It is a light thing that thou shouldest be my servant to raise up the tribes of Jacob------I will also give thee for a light to the Gentiles, that thou may'st be my salvation unto the end of the earth.* Isaiah liv. *v.* 1, 2, 3. *Sing, O barren, thou that didst not bear, break forth into singing, and cry aloud that thou didst not travel with child; for more are the children of the desolate, than the children of the married wife, saith the Lord. Enlarge the place of thy tent, and let them stretch forth the curtains of thy habitation: spare not, lengthen thy cords and strengthen thy stakes: for thou shalt break forth on the right hand and on the left; and thy seed shall inherit the Gentiles, &c.* Malachi i. *v.* 11. *From the rising of the sun even to the going down of the same my name shall be great among the Gentiles.* See Isaiah ii. *v.* 2, 3. Micah iv. *v.* 1, 2. Daniel ii. *v.* 13, &c.

SECT. 5. *That the Church of* Christ *must be* Apostolical, *by a Succession of her Pastors, and a lawful Mission derived from the Apostles.*

Q. *How do you prove this?*

*A.* 1st, Because only those that can derive their Lineage from the Apostles are the Heirs of the Apostles: And consequently they alone can claim a Right to the Scriptures, to the Administration of the Sacraments, or any Share in the Pastoral Ministry: 'Tis their proper Inheritance, which they have received from the Apostles, and the Apostles from *Christ. As my Father hath sent me, even so I send you.* John xx. *v.* 21.  B  2dly,

2*dly*, Becaufe *Chrift* promifed to the Apoftles and their Succeffors, *that he would be with them always even to the end of the world*, Matt. xxviii. *v.* 20. and that the Holy Ghoft, *the Jpirit of truth, fhould abide with them for ever*, John xiv. *v.* 16, 17.

## Sect. 6. *That* Catholicks, *and not* Proteftants, *are the true Church of* Chrift.

Q. *How do you prove that the* Catholick *Church in Communion with* Rome, *is the true Church of* Chrift, *rather than* Proteftants *or other Sectaries?*

*A.* From what has been already faid in the foregoing *Sections:* For, 1*ft*, The true Church of *Chrift* can be no other than that which has always had a vifible Being in the World ever fince *Chrift's* Time; as we have feen *Sect.* 1. She was founded by *Chrift* himfelf, with exprefs Promife, *that the gates of hell fhould not prevail againft her*, Matt. xvi. *v.* 18. *She is the kingdom of Chrift which fhall never be deftroyed*, Dan. ii. *v.* 44. Therefore the true Church of *Chrift* can be no other than the *Catholick*, which alone has always had a vifible Being in the World ever fince *Chrift's* Time: Not the *Proteftant*, or any other modern Sect, which only came into the World fince the Year 1500. For thofe that came into the World 1500 Years after *Chrift*, came into the World 1500 Years too late to be the Religion or Church of *Chrift*.

2*dly*, The true Church of *Chrift*, in virtue of the Promife both of the *Old* and *New Teftament*, was to continue pure and holy in her Doctrine and Terms of Communion in all Ages, even to the End of the World, as we have feen *Sect.* 3. and confequently could never ftand in need of a *Proteftant* Reformation: Therefore that which was of old the true Church of *Chrift* muft ftill be fo; and it is vain to feek for the true Church among any of the Sects of Pretenders to Reformation; becaufe they all build upon

a wrong

a wrong Foundation, that is, upon the Suppofition that the Church of *Chrift* was for many Ages gone aftray.

3*dly*, The true Church of *Chrift* muft be *Catholick*, or Univerfal; fhe muft not only be the Church of all Ages, but alfo more or lefs the Church of all Nations, as we have feen *Sect.* 4. She muft be *Apoftolical*, by a Succeffion and Miffion derived from the Apoftles, as we alfo have feen *Sect.* 5. Now thefe Characters cannot agree to any of our modern Sects, but only to the old Religion, which alone is the Church of all Ages, and more or lefs of all Nations; and which defcends in an uninterrupted Succeffion continued in the fame Communion from the Apoftles down to thefe our Days. Therefore the old Religion alone is the true Church of *Chrift:* Which can be but one, and in one Communion, as we have feen *Sect.* 2.

✥✥✥✥✥✥✥✥✥✥✥✥✥✥✥✥✥✥✥✥✥✥✥

# C H A P.  II.

## *Of Scripture and Tradition.*

Q. *W*HAT *is your Belief concerning the Scripture?*
*A.* That it is to be received by all *Chriftians* as the infallible Word of God.

Q. *Do you look upon the Scripture to be clear and plain in all Points* neceffary; *that is, in all fuch Points wherein our Salvation is fo far concern'd, that the mifunderftanding and mifinterpreting of it may endanger our eternal Welfare?*

*A.* No: Becaufe St. *Peter* affures us, 2 *Pet.* iii. *v.* 16. That in St. *Paul*'s Epiftle *there are fome things hard to be underftood, which they that are unlearned and unftable wreft, as they do alfo the other fcriptures, to their own deftruction.*

Q. *How then is this Danger to be avoided?*

*A.* By taking the Meaning and Interpretation of the Scripture from the fame Hand, from which we received the Book itfelf, that is, from the Church.

Q. *Why may not every particular* Chriftian *have Liberty to interpret the Scripture according to his own private Judgment, without Regard to the Interpretation of the Church?*

*A.* 1*ft*, Becaufe *no prophecy of the fcripture is of private interpretation*, 2 *Pet.* i. *v.* 20.　2*dly*, Becaufe as Men's Judgments are as different as their Faces, fuch Liberty as this muft needs produce as many Religions almoft as Men.　3*dly*, Becaufe *Chrift* has left his Church, and her Paftors and Teachers, to be our Guides in all Controverfies relating to Religion, and confequently in the underftanding of holy Writ. *Eph.* iv. *v.* 11, 12, &c. *He gave fome apoftles, and fome prophets, and fome evangelifts, and fome paftors and teachers, for the perfecting of the faints, for the work of the miniftry, for the edifying of the body of Chrift, till we all come in the unity of the faith and of the knowledge of the Son of God unto a perfect man, unto the meafure of the ftature of the fulnefs of Chrift. That we henceforth be no more children toffed to and fro, and carried about with every wind of doctrine, by the flight of men and cunning craftinefs, whereby they lie in wait to deceive; but fpeaking the truth in love, may grow up in him in all things which is the head, even Chrift.* Hence St. *John*, in his firft *Epiftle, Chap.* iv. *v.* 6. gives us this Rule, for the trying of Spirits. *He that knoweth God, heareth us;* [the Paftors of the Church] *he that is not of God, heareth not us: by this we know the fpirit of truth, and the fpirit of error.*

Q. *Why does the Church in her Profeffion of Faith, oblige her Children never to take or interpret the Scripture otherwife than according to the unanimous Confent of the holy Fathers?*

*A.* To arm them againft Danger of Novelty and Error: *Proverbs* xxii. *v.* 28. *Remove not the ancient land-mark which thy fathers have fet.*

SECT.

SECT. 2. *Of Apostolical and Ecclesiastical Tradition.*

Q. *What do you mean by Apostolical Traditions?*

*A.* All such Points of Faith, or Church Discipline, which were taught, or establish'd by the Apostles, and have carefully been preserved in the Church ever since.

Q. *What Difference is there between* Apostolical *and* Ecclesiastical *Traditions?*

*A.* The Difference is this, that *Apostolical Traditions* are those which had their Original or Institution from the Apostles: Such as Infants Baptism, the Lord's Day, receiving the Sacrament fasting, &c. *Ecclesiastical Traditions* are such as had their Institution from the Church, as Holidays and Fasts ordain'd by the Church.

Q. *How are we to know what* Traditions *are truly* Apostolical, *and what not?*

*A.* In the same Manner, and by the same Authority, by which we know what Scriptures are Apostolical, and what not: That is, by the Authority of the Apostolical Church guided by the unerring Spirit of God.

Q. *But why should not the Scripture alone be the Rule of our Faith, without having Recourse to Apostolical Tradition?*

*A.* 1. Because, without the Help of Apostolical Tradition, we cannot so much as tell what is Scripture, and what is not. 2. Because Infants Baptism and several other necessary Articles are either not at all contain'd in Scripture, or at least are not plain in the Scripture, without the Help of Tradition.

Q. *What Scripture can you bring in Favour of Tradition?*

*A. Therefore brethren stand fast, and hold the traditions, which ye have been taught, whether by word or our epistle,* 2 Theff. ii. v. 15. *Ask thy father, and he will shew thee, thy elders, and they will tell*

*thee,*

*thee,* Deut. xxxii. *v.* 7. *See* Pfal. xix. *v.* 5, 6, 7.
1 Cor. xi. *v.* 2. 2 Theff. iii. *v.* 6. 2 Tim. i.
*v.* 13. *C.* ii. *v.* 2. *C.* iii. *v.* 14.

SECT. 3. *Of the Ordinance and Conftitutions of the Church.*

Q. *Why do you make Profeffion of admitting and embracing all the Ordinances and Conftitutions of the Church ?*

*A.* Becaufe *Chrift* has fo commanded. *He that heareth you, heareth me, and he that defpifeth you, de-fpifeth me,* Luke x. *v.* 16. *As my father hath fent me, even fo I fend you,* John xx. *v.* 21. Hence St. *Paul,* Heb. xiii. *v.* 17. tells us, *Obey them that have the rule over you, and fubmit yourfelves.*

Q. *Why does the Church command fo many Holidays to be kept ? Is it not enough to keep the* Sunday *holy ?*

*A.* God in the old Law did not think it enough to appoint the weekly *Sabbath,* which was the *Satur-day :* But alfo ordain'd feveral other Feftivals, as that of the *Paffover,* in Memory of the Delivery of his People from the *Egyptian* Bondage, that of the *Weeks* or *Pentecoft,* that of *Tabernacles, &c.* and the Church has done the fame in the new Law, to celebrate the Memory of the chief Myfteries of our Redemption, and to blefs God in his Saints. And in this *Proteftants* feem to agree with us, by appointing almoft all the fame Holidays in their Common-Prayer-Book.

Q. *Is it not faid in the Law,* Exod. xx. *v.* 9. Six days fhalt thou labour and do all thy work, *&c. Why then fhould the Church derogate from this Part of the Commandment ?*

*A.* This was to be underftood in cafe no Holiday came in the Week; otherwife the Law would con-tradict itfelf, when in the 23d Chap. of *Leviticus* it appoints fo many other Holidays befides the *Sabbath,*
with

with Command to abſtain from all ſervile Work on them.

Q. *As to faſting Days, do you look upon it ſinful to eat Meat on thoſe Days without Neceſſity?*

*A.* Yes: Becauſe it is a Sin to diſobey the Church: *If he neglect to hear the church, let him be to thee as a heathen and a publican.* Matt. xviii. *v.* 17.

Q. *Does not* Chriſt *ſay,* Matt. xv. *v.* 11. That which goeth into the Mouth doth not defile a Man?

*A.* True: 'Tis not any Uncleanneſs in the Meat, as many ancient Hereticks imagin'd, or any Dirt or Duſt which may ſtick to it by eating it without firſt waſhing the Hands, (of which Caſe our Lord ſpeaks in the Text here quoted) which can defile the Soul: For every Creature of God is good, and whatſoever corporal Filth enters in at the Mouth is caſt forth into the Draught: But that which defiles the Soul, when a Perſon eats Meat on a faſting Day, is the Diſobedience of the Heart, in tranſgreſſing the Precept of the Church of God. In like Manner, when *Adam* eat of the forbidden Fruit, it was not the Apple which entered in by the Mouth, but the Diſobedience to the Law of God which defiled him.

❀❀❀❀❀❀❀❀❀❀❀❀❀❀❀❀❀❀❀❀❀❀

# C H A P. III.

## *Of the Sacraments.*

Q. *W H A T do you mean by a Sacrament?*

*A.* An Inſtitution of *Chriſt*, conſiſting in ſome outward Sign or Ceremony, by which Grace is given to the Soul of the worthy Receiver.

Q. *How many ſuch Sacraments do you find in Scripture?*

*A.* Theſe Seven; *Baptiſm, Confirmation, Euchariſt,* (which *Proteſtants* call *the Lord's Supper*) *Penance, Extreme Unction* (or the Anointing of the Sick) *Holy Orders,* and *Matrimony.*                    Q. *What*

Q. *What Scripture have you for Baptifm?*

*A.* John iii. *v.* 5. *Except a man be born of water and of the fpirit, he cannot enter the Kingdom of God.* Matt. xxviii. *v.* 19. *Go teach all nations, baptizing them in the name of the Father, and of the Son, and of the Holy Ghoft.*

Q. *How do you prove that this Commiffion given to the Apoftles of baptizing all Nations, is to be underflood of Baptifm adminifter'd in Water ?*

*A.* From the Belief and Practice of the Church of *Chrift* in all Ages, and of the Apoftles themfelves ; who adminifter'd Baptifm in Water : *Acts* viii. *v.* 36, 38. *See here is water,* faid the Eunoch to St. *Philip, what does hinder me to be baptized ?----And they went down both into the water, both* Philip *and the Eunech; and he baptized him.* Acts x. *v.* 47, 48. *Can any man forbide water,* faid St. *Peter, that thefe fhould not be baptized, which have received the Holy Ghoft as well as we ? And he commanded them to be baptized in the name of the Lord.*

Q. *What do you mean by Confirmation ?*

*A.* Confirmation is a Sacrament, wherein, by the Invocation of the Holy Ghoft, and Impofition of the Bifhop's Hands with the Unction of Holy Chrifm, a Perfon receives the Grace of the H. Ghoft, and a Strength in order to the Profeffion of his Faith.

Q. *What Scripture have you for Confirmation ?*

*A. Acts* viii. 15, 17. Where *Peter* and *John* confirm'd the *Samaritans. They pray'd for them that they might receive the Holy Ghoft.--Then laid they their hands on them, and they received the Holy Ghoft.*

Q. *What Scripture have you for the* Eucharift, *or* Supper of the Lord.

*A.* We have the Hiftory of its Inftitution fet down at large, *Mat.* xxvi. *Mar.* xiv. *Luke* xxii. 1 *Cor.* xi. And that this Sacrament was to be continued in the Church *till the Lord comes,* that is, till the Day of Judgment, we learn from St. *Paul,* 1 *Cor.* xi. *v.* 26.

Q. *What*

Q. *What do you mean by the Sacrament of Penance?*

*A.* The Confeſſion of Sins with a ſincere Repent-ance, and the Prieſt's Abſolution.

Q. *What Scripture have you to prove that the Bi-ſhops and Prieſts of the Church have Power to abſolve the Sinner that confeſſes his Sins with a ſincere Re-pentance?*

*A.* John xx. *v.* 22, 23. *Receive ye the H. Ghoſt: Whoſeſoever ſins ye remit, they are remitted unto them: And whoſeſoever ſins ye retain, they are retained.* Matt. xviii. *v.* 18. *Verily I ſay unto you, Whatſoever ye ſhall bind on earth ſhall be bound in heaven: And whatſoever ye ſhall looſe on earth ſhall be looſed in heaven.* Which Texts *Proteſtants* ſeem to underſtand in the ſame Manner as we, ſince, in their Common-Prayer-Book, in the *Order for the Viſitation of the Sick*, we find this Rubrick: *Here ſhall the ſick Perſon be moved to make a ſpecial Confeſſion of his Sins, if he feels his Conſcience troubled with any weighty Matter. After which Con-feſſion the Prieſt ſhall abſolve him (if he humbly and heartily deſire it) after this Sort:*

Our Lord *Jeſus Chriſt*, who hath left Power to his Church to abſolve all Sinners who truly repent and believe in him, of his great Mercy forgive thee thine Offences: And by this Authority committed to me, I abſolve thee from all thy Sins, In the Name of the Fa-ther, and of the Son, and of the H. Ghoſt. *Amen.*

Q. *How do you prove from the Texts above quoted of* John xx. *v.* 22, 23. *and* Matt. xviii. *v.* 18. *The Ne-ceſſity of the Faithful confeſſing their Sins to the Paſtors of the Church, in order to obtain the Abſolution and Remiſſion of them?*

*A.* Becauſe in the Texts above quoted *Chriſt* has made the Paſtors of his Church his *Judges* in the Court of Conſcience, with Commiſſion and Authority to *bind* or to *looſe*, to *forgive* or to *retain Sins*, accord-ing to the Merits of the Cauſe, and the Diſpoſition of the Penitents. Now as no Judge can paſs Sentence
with-

without having a full Knowledge of the Caufe; which cannot be had in this Kind of Caufes, which regard Men's Confciences, but by their own Confeffion; it clearly follows, that he who has made the Paftors of his Church, the Judges of Men's Confciences, has alfo laid an Obligation upon the Faithful to lay open the State of their Confciences to them, if they hope to have their Sins remitted. Nor would our Lord have given to h.s Church the Power of *retaining Sins*, much lefs the *keys of the kingdom of heaven*, Matt. xvi. *v.* 19. if fuch Sins as exclude Men from the Kingdom of Heaven might be remitted independently of the Keys of the Church.

Q. *Have you any other Texts of Scripture, which favour the* Catholick *Doctrine and Practice of Confeffion ?*

A. Yes, We find in the old Law, which was a Figure of the Law of *Chrift*, that fuch as were infected with the Leprofy, which was a Figure of Sin, were obliged to fhew themfelves to the Priefts, and fubject themfelves to their Judgment. See *Lev.* xiii. and xiv. and *Matt.* viii. *v.* 4. Which, according to the holy Fathers, was an Emblem of the Confeffion of Sins in the Sacrament of Penance. And in the fame Law a fpecial Confeffion of Sins was exprefsly prefcribed. *Numb.* v. *v.* 6, 7. *When a man or Woman fhall commit any fin that men commit, to do a trefpafs againft the Lord, and that perfon be guilty, then they fhall confefs their fin which they have done.* The fame is prefcribed in the New Teftament, *James* v. *v.* 16. *Confefs your faults one to another*; that is, to the Priefts or Elders of the Church, whom the Apoftle had order'd to be call'd for, *v.* 14. And this was evidently the Practice of the firft Chriftians. *Acts* xix. *v.* 18. *Many that believed, came and confeffed, and fhew'd their Deeds.*

Q. *What do you mean by* Extreme Unction ?

A. You

*A.* You have both the full Defcription and Proof of it. *James* v. *v.* 14, 15. *Is any fick among you, let him call for the elders (the priefts) of the church and let them pray over him, anointing him with oil in the name of the Lord: And the prayer of faith fhall fave the fick, and the Lord fhall raife him up ; and if he have committed fins, they fhall be forgiven him.*

Q. *What is* Holy Order ?

*A.* A Sacrament inftituted by *Chrift*, by which Bifhops, Priefts, &c. are confecrated to their refpective Functions, and receive Grace to difcharge them well.

Q. *When did* Chrift *inftitute the Sacrament of* Holy Order ?

*A.* At his laft Supper, when he made his Apoftles Priefts, by giving them the Power of confecrating the Bread and Wine into his Body and Blood, *Luke* xxii. *v.* 19. *Do this in remembrance of me.* To which he added, after his Refurrection, the Power of forgiving the Sins of the Penitent, *John* xx. *v.* 22, 23.

Q. *What Scripture Proof have you that* Holy Orders *give Grace to thofe that receive them worthily ?*

*A.* The Words of St. *Paul* to *Timothy,* whom he had ordained Prieft by Impofition of Hands, 2 *Tim.* i. *v.* 6. *Stir up the gift of God, which is in thee by the putting on of my hands*; and 1 *Tim.* iv. *v.* 14. *Neglect not the gift that is in thee, which was given thee by prophecy, by the laying on of the hands of the prefbytery.*

Q. *When was Matrimony inftituted ?*

*A.* It was firft inftituted by God Almighty in Paradife between our firft Parents; and this Inftitution was confirmed by *Chrift* in the new Law. *Matt.* xix. *v.* 4, 5, 6. where he concludes. *What God hath joined together let no man put afunder.*

Q. *How do you prove that Matrimony is a Sacrament ?*

*A.* Becaufe it is a Conjunction made and fanctified by God himfelf, and not to be diffolv'd by any

Power

Power of Man; as being a facred Sign, or myfterious
Reprefentation of the indiffoluble Union of *Chrift*
and his Church. *Ephef.* v. *v.* 31, 32. *For this caufe
fhall a man leave his father and mother, and fhall be joined to his wife, and they two fhall be one flefh. This is a
great myftery (a Sacrament) but I fpeak concerning*
Chrift *and the church,* (in Chrift *and in the church.*)

Q. *Why does the church not allow of the Marriage
of the Clergy?*

*A.* Becaufe upon their entering into Holy Orders,
they make a Vow, or folemn Promife, to God and the
Church, to live continently; now the Breach of fuch
a Vow as this would be a great Sin; witnefs St. *Paul,*
1 Tim. v. *v.* 11, 22. where fpeaking of Widows
that are for marrying, after having made fuch a Vow
as this, he fays, they *have damnation becaufe they have
caft off their firft faith,* that is, their folemn Engage-
ment made with God.

Q. *But why does the Church receive none to Holy
Orders, but thofe that make this Vow?*

*A.* Becaufe fhe does not think it proper, that they,
who by their Office and Functions ought to be wholly
devoted to the Service of God, and the Care of Souls,
fhould be diverted from thefe Duties by the Diftracti-
ons of a married Life, 1 *Cor.* viii. *v.* 32, 33. *He that
is unmarried careth for the things that belong to the
Lord, how he may pleafe the Lord.    But he that is married, careth for the things that are of the world, how he
may pleafe his wife.*

Q. *Why does the Church make ufe of fo many Ceremonies in adminiftering the Sacraments?*

*A.* To ftir up Devotion in the People, and Reverence to the facred Myfteries; to inftruct the
Faithful concerning the Effects and Graces given by
the Sacraments; and to perform Things relating to
God's Honour and Salvation of Souls with a becom-
ing Decency.

Q. *Have*

Q. *Have you any Warrant from Scripture for the Use of such Ceremonies?*

*A.* Yes: We have the Example of *Christ*, who frequently used the like Ceremonies. For instance, in curing the man that was deaf and dumb, *Mark* vii. *v.* 33, 34. In curing him that was born blind, *John* ix. *v.* 6, 7. In breathing upon his Apostles when he gave them the Holy Ghost, *John* xx. *v.* 22, &c.

## CHAP. IV.

### *Of the Real Presence and Transubstantiation.*

Q. *WHAT is the Doctrine of the* Catholick *Church in relation to this Article?*

*A.* We believe and profess, *That in the most holy Sacrament of the Eucharist, there is truly, really and substantially the Body and Blood, together with the Soul and Divinity of our Lord* Jesus Christ. *And that there is a Conversion (or Change) of the whole Substance of the Bread into his Body, and of the whole Substance of the Wine into his Blood: Which Conversion (or Change) the* Catholick *Church calls Transubstantiation.*

Q. *What Proofs have you for this?*

*A.* 1st, Matt. xxvi. *v.* 26. *As they were eating, Jesus took bread and blessed it, and break it, and gave it to the disciples, and said, Take, eat;* THIS IS MY BODY. *And he took the cup, and gave thanks, and gave it to them, saying, Drink ye all of it.* FOR THIS IS MY BLOOD OF THE NEW TESTAMENT WHICH IS SHED FOR MANY FOR THE REMISSION OF SINS. Mark xiv. *v.* 22, 24. *Take, eat; This is my body---This is my blood of the new testament which is shed for many.* Luke xxii. *v.* 19. *This is my body which is given for you: this do in remembrance of me.*

C                                    ---*This*

---*This cup is the new testament in my blood which is shed for you.* 1 Cor. xi. *v.* 24, 25. *Take, eat; This is my blood which is broken for you---This cup is the new testament in my blood.* Which Words of *Christ*, repeated in so many Places, cannot be verified, without offering Violence to the Text, any other Way than by a real Change of the Bread and Wine into his Body and Blood.

2*dly*, 1 Cor. x. *v.* 16 *The cup of blessing which we bless, is it not the communion of the blood of Christ? The bread which we break, is it not the communion of the body of Christ?* Which Interrogation of the Apostle is certainly equivalent to an Affirmation; and evidently declares, that in the blessed Sacrament we really receive the Body and Blood of *Christ*.

3*dly*, 1 Cor. xi. *v.* 27, 29. *Whosoever shall eat this bread or drink the cup of the Lord unworthily, shall be* GUILTY OF THE BODY AND BLOOD OF THE LORD---*He that eateth and drinketh unworthily, eateth and drinketh damnation to himself,* NOT DISCERNING THE BODY OF OUR LORD. Now how should a Person be *guilty of the Body and Blood of the Lord,* by receiving unworthily, if what he received were only Bread and Wine, and not *the Body and Blood of our Lord?* Or where should be the Crime of *not discerning the Body of our Lord,* if the *Body of our Lord* were not there?

4*thly*, John vi. *v.* 51, &*c.* *The bread that I will give is my flesh, which I will give for the life of the world. The Jews therefore strove amongst themselves, saying, How can this Man give us his flesh to eat? Then Jesus said unto them, Verily, verily, I say unto you, except ye eat the flesh of the Son of man, and drink his blood, ye have no life in you. Whoso eateth my flesh, and drinketh my blood, hath eternal life, and I will raise him up at the last Day.* FOR MY FLESH IS MEAT INDEED, AND MY BLOOD IS DRINK INDEED. *He that eateth my flesh, and drinketh my blood,*

*blood, dwelleth in me, and I in him. As the living Father hath sent me, and I live by the Father: so he that eateth me, even he shall live by me.* This is *that bread which came down from heaven, not as your fathers did eat manna and are dead: he that eateth of this bread shall live for ever.*

Hence the *Protestants*, in their Catechism in the Common-Prayer-Book, are forced to acknowledge *that the Body and Blood of* Christ *are* verily *and indeed taken and received by the Faithful in the Lord's Supper.* Now how that can be *verily and indeed taken and receiv'd* which is not *verily and indeed* there, is a greater Mystery than Transubstantiation.

*The literal Sense is hard to Flesh and Blood:
But Nonsense never can be understood.*
Dryden *Hind.* and *Panth.*

Q. *Are we not commanded,* Luke xxii. *v.* 19. *to receive the Sacrament in* remembrance *of Christ?*

*A.* Yes, we are: And St. *Paul,* 1 Cor. xi. *v.* 26. lets us know what it is that is to be the Object of our Remembrance when we receive, when he tells us, *Ye do shew* (or *shew forth*) *the Lord's Death till he comes.* But this *Remembrance* is no ways opposite to the real Presence of *Christ*'s Body and Blood: On the contrary, what better Remembrance can there be of *Christ*'s Death and Passion, than to receive under the sacramental Veils the same Body and Blood in which he suffered for us?

Q. *Why then do you blame* Protestants *for taking this Sacrament in* Remembrance *of* Christ?

*A.* We don't blame them for taking it in *Remembrance* of him: But we blame them for taking it as a *bare Remembrance,* so as to exclude the Reality of his Body and Blood. That is, we blame them for taking the *Remembrance* and leaving out the Substance; whereas the Words of *Christ* require that they should acknowledge both.

C 2
Q. *But*

Q. *But how is it possible that the Sacrament should contain the real Body and Blood of* Christ.

*A.* Because nothing is impossible to the Almighty; and it is the highest Rashness, not to say Blasphemy, for poor Worms of the Earth to dispute the Power of God.

✤✤✤✤✤✤✤✤✤✤✤✤✤✤✤✤✤✤✤✤✤

## C H A P  V.

### *Of Communion in one Kind.*

Q. *WHAT is the Doctrine of the Church as to this Point ?*

*A.* We profess, *that under either Kind alone* Christ *is received whole and entire, and a true Sacrament.*

Q. *What Proof have you for this ?*

*A.* Because, as we have seen in the foregoing Chapter, the Bread by Consecration is truly and really changed into the Body of *Christ*, and the Wine into his Blood : Now both Faith and Reason tell us, that the living Body of the Son of God cannot be without his Blood, nor his Blood without his Body : Nor his Body and Blood without his Soul and Divinity. 'Tis true, he shed his Blood for us in his Passion ; and his Soul at his Death was parted from his Body : But now he is risen from the Dead immortal and impassible, and can shed his Blood no more, nor die any more. *Christ being raised from the dead*, says the Apostle, *Rom.* vi. *v.* 9. *dieth no more; death hath no more dominion over him.* Therefore whosoever receives the Body of *Christ*, receives *Christ* himself whole and entire; there is no receiving him by Parts.

Q. *But does not* Christ *say,* John vi. *v.* 53. Except ye eat the flesh of the Son of man, and drink his blood, ye have no life in you ?

*A.* True.

*A.* True. But according to the *Catholick* Doctrine we do this, tho' we receive under one Kind alone, becaufe under either Kind we receive both the Body and Blood of *Chriſt :* Whereas our Adverſaries that make this Objection receive neither one nor the other, but only a little Bread and Wine. Beſides, this Objection does not found well in *Proteſtant* Mouths, becauſe they ſay thoſe Words of *Chriſt* were not ſpoken of the Sacrament, but only of Faith.

Q. *Are not all* Chriſtians *commanded to drink of the Cup,* Mat. xxvi. *v.* 27. Drink ye all of it.

*A.* No : that Command was only addreſs'd to the twelve Apoſtles, who were *the all* that were then preſent, *and they all drank of it,* Mark xiv. *v.* 23.

Q. *How do you prove, that thoſe Words are not to be underſtood as a Command directed to all* Chriſtians ?

*A.* Becauſe the Church of *Chriſt,* which is the beſt Interpreter of his Word, never underſtood them ſo ; and therefore from the very Beginning, on many Occaſions, ſhe gave the Holy Communion in one Kind, for inſtance, to Children, to the Sick, to the Faithful in Time of Perſecution, to be carried Home with them, *&c.* as appears from the moſt certain Monuments of Antiquity.

Q. *But are not the Faithful thus deprived of a great Part of the Grace of this Sacrament.*

*A.* No ; becauſe under one Kind they receive the ſame as they would do under both ; inſomuch as they receive *Chriſt* himſelf whole and entire, the Author and Fountain of all Graces.

Q. *Why then ſhould the Prieſt in the Maſs receive in both Kinds any more than the reſt of the Faithful ?*

*A.* Becauſe the Maſs being a Sacrifice, in which, by the Inſtitution of our Lord, the ſhedding of his Blood and his Death was to be in a lively Manner

C 3                          repreſented ;

reprefented; it is requifite that the Prieft, who as
the Minifter of *Chrift* offers this Sacrifice, fhould,
for the more lively reprefenting of the Separation of
*Chrift*'s Blood from his Body, confecrate and receive
in both Kinds, as often as he fays Mafs. Whereas
at other Times, neither Prieft, nor Bifhop, nor Pope
himfelf, even upon their Death-bed, receives any
otherwife than the reft of the Faithful, *viz.* in one
Kind only.

Q. *Have you any Texts of Scripture that favour
Communion in one Kind?*

*A.* Yes.    *1ft,* All fuch Texts as promife everlafting Life to them that receive, tho' but in *one
Kind*; as John vi. *v.* 51. *The bread that I will
give is my flefh, which I will give for the life of the
world.* V. 57. *He that eateth me, even he fhall live
by me.* V. 58. *He that eateth of this bread, fhall
live for ever.*

*2dly,* All fuch Texts as make mention of the
Faithful receiving the Holy Communion, under the
Name of *Breaking of Bread,* without any mention
of the Cup; as, Acts ii. *v.* 24. *They continued
ftedfaftly in the apoftles doctrine and fellowfhip, and
in breaking of bread and in prayers.* V. 46. *Conti-
nuing daily with one accord in the temple, and breaking
bread from houfe to houfe.* Acts xx. *v.* 7. *Upon the
firft day of the week, when the difciples came together to
break bread.* Luke xxiv. *v.* 30, 31. *He took bread
and bleffed it, and brake, and gave to them, and their
eyes were opened, and they knew him, and he vanifhed
out of their fight.* 1 Cor. xi. *v.* ☛. *We being many,
are one bread, and one body, for we are all partakers
of that one bread.*

*3dly,* 1 Cor. xi. *v* 27. Where the Apoftle declares, that whofoever receives under either Kind
unworthily, is guilty both of the Body and Blood
of *Chrift. Whofoever fhall eat this bread,* or *drink*

(ἡ πίνῃ) *this cup of the Lord unworthily, shall be guilty of the body and blood of our Lord.* Where the *Protestant* Tranflations have evidently corrupted the Text by putting in *and drink* inftead of *or drink*, as it is in the Original.

Q. *What are the Reafons why the Church does not give the Communion to all her Children in both Kinds?*

A. 1*ft*, Becaufe of the Danger of fpilling the Blood of *Chrift*, which could hardly be avoided, if all were to receive the Cup. 2*dly*, Becaufe, confidering how foon Wine decays, the Sacrament could not well be kept for the Sick in both Kinds. 3*dly*, Becaufe fome Conftitutions can neither endure the Tafte nor Smell of Wine. 4*thly*, Becaufe true Wine in fome Countries is very hard to be met with. 5*thly*, In fine, in oppofition to thofe Hereticks that deny that *Chrift* is receiv'd whole and entire under either Kind.

❖❖❖❖❖❖❖❖❖❖❖❖❖❖❖❖❖❖❖❖❖❖❖

## CHAP VI.

### Of the Mafs.

Q. *WHAT is the* Catholick *Doctrine as to the Mafs?*

A. That *in the Mafs there is offer'd to God a true, proper and propitiatory Sacrifice for the Living and the Dead.*

Q. *What do you mean by the Mafs?*

A. The Confecration and Oblation of the Body and Blood of *Chrift* under the facramental Veils or Appearances of Bread and Wine: So that the Mafs was inftituted by *Chrift* himfelf at his laft Supper: *Chrift* himfelf faid the firft Mafs; and ordain'd that his Apoftles and their Succeffors fhould do the like, *Do this in remembrance of me*, Luke xxii. 19.

Q. *What do you mean by a* propitiatory *Sacrifice?*

A. A

*A.* A Sacrifice for obtaining *Mercy*, or by which God is moved to *Mercy*.

*Q.* How do you prove that the Mafs is fuch a Sacrifice ?

*A.* Becaufe in the Mafs *Chrift* himfelf, as we have feen, *chap.* iv. is really prefent, and by Virtue of the Confecration, is there exhibited and prefented to the eternal Father under the facramental Veils, which, by their feparate Confecration, reprefent his Death. Now what can more move God to Mercy, than the Oblation of his only Son there really prefent, and under this Figure of Death reprefenting to his Father that Death which he fuffered for us ?

*Q.* What Scripture do you bring for this ?

*A.* The Words of Confecration, as they are related by St. *Luke,* Chap. xxii. *v.* 19, 20. *This is my body, which is given for you---This cup is the new teftament in my blood which* (Cup) *is fhed for you.* For if the Cup be fhed for us, that is, for our Sins, it muft need be *Propitiatory,* at leaft by applying to us the Fruits of the *bloody Sacrifice* of the Crofs.

*Q.* What other Text of the Scripture do the Fathers apply to the Sacrifice of the Mafs ?

*A.* 1*ft,* The Words of God in the firft Chapter of the Prophet *Malach. v.* 10, 11. where, rejecting the *Jewifh* Sacrifices, he declares his Acceptance of that Sacrifice, or *pure Offering,* which fhould be made to him in every Place among the *Gentiles.* 2*dly,* Thofe Words of the Pfalmift, *Pf.* cx *v.* 4. *Thou art a prieft for ever, according to the order of* Melchifedech : Why according to the Order of *Melchifedeck,* fay the holy Fathers, but by Reafon of the Sacrifice of the Eucharift prefigur'd by that Bread and Wine offer'd by *Melchifedech,* Gen. xiv. *v.* 18.

*Q.* Why does the Church celebrate the Mafs in the Latin, which the People, for the moft Part do not underftand ?

*A.* 1*ft.*

*A.* 1*st.* Because it is the ancient Language of the Church used in the publick Liturgy in all Ages in the western Parts of the World. 2*dly*, For a greater Uniformity in the publick Worship; that so a *Christian,* in whatsoever Country he chances to be, may still find the Liturgy performed in the same Manner, and in the same Language, to which he is accustomed at Home. 3*dly,* To avoid the Changes which all vulgar Languages are daily exposed to. 4*thly,* Because the Mass being a Sacrifice which the Priest, as Minister of *Christ,* is to offer, and the Prayers of the Mass being mostly fitted for this End, it is enough that they be in a Language which he understands. Nor is this any ways injurious to the People, who are instructed to accompany him in every Part of this Sacrifice, by Prayers accommodated to their Devotion, which they have in their ordinary Prayer-Books.

Q. *What is the best Manner of hearing Mass?*

*A.* The Mass being instituted for a standing Memorial of *Christ's* Death and Passion, and being in Substance the same Sacrifice as that which *Christ* offer'd upon the Cross, because both the Priest and the Victim is the same *Jesus Christ*; there can be no better Manner of hearing Mass than by meditating on the Death and Passion of *Christ* their represented; and putting one's self in the same Dispositions of Faith, Love, Repentance, *&c.* as we should have endeavoured to excite in ourselves, had we been present at his Passion and Death on Mount *Calvary?*

Q. *What are the Ends for which this Sacrifice is offered to God?*

*A.* Principally these four, which both Priest and People ought to have in View. 1. For God's own Honour and Glory. 2. In Thankfgiving for all his Blessings conferr'd on us, thro' *Jesus Christ* our Lord. 3. In Satisfaction for our Sins, thro' his Blood. 4. For obtaining Grace and all necessary Blessings from God.

CHAP.

## CHAP. VII.

### *Of Purgatory.*

Q. *WHAT is the Doctrine of the Church as to this Point ?*

*A.* We *constantly hold that there is a Purgatory, and that the Souls therein detained are helped by the Suffrages of the Faithful :* That is, by the Prayers and Alms offered for them, and principally by the holy Sacrifice of the Mass.

Q. *What do you mean by Purgatory ?*

*A.* A middle State of Souls which depart this Life in God's Grace, yet not without some lesser Stains or Guilt of Punishment, which retards them from entering Heaven. But as to the particular Place where these Souls suffer, or the Quality of the Torments which they suffer, the Church has decided nothing.

Q. *What Sort of* Christians *then go to Purgatory ?*

*A.* 1*st*, Such as die guilty of lesser Sins, which we commonly call *Venial*; as many Christians do, who, either by sudden Death, or otherwise, are taken out of this Life before they have repented for these ordinary Failings. 2*dly*, Such as having been formerly guilty of greater Sins, have not made full Satisfaction for them to the divine Justice.

Q. *Why do you say that those who die guilty of lesser Sins go to Purgatory ?*

*A.* Because such as depart this Life before they have repented for these venial Frailties and Imperfections, cannot be supposed to be condemn'd to the eternal Torments of Hell, since the Sins of which they are guilty are but small, which even God's best Servants are more or less liable to. Nor can they go strait to Heaven in this State, because the Scripture assures us, *Revelat.* xxi. *v.* 27. *There shall in no wise enter thither any thing that defileth.*
Now

Now every Sin, be it ever fo fmall, certainly *defileth* the Soul. Hence our Saviour affures us, that we are to render an Account *even for every idle word.* Matt. xii. *v.* 36.

*Q* *Upon what then do you ground your Belief of* Purgatory?

*A.* Upon Scripture, Tradition, and Reafon.

Q. *How upon Scripture?*

*A.* Becaule the Scripture in many Places affures us, that *God will render to every one according to his works,* Pf. lxii. *v.* 12. Matt. xvi. *v.* 27. Rom. ii. *v.* 6. Revel. xxii. *v.* 12. Now this would not be true, if there were no fuch Thing as Purgatory; for how would God render to every one according to his Works, if fuch as die in the Guilt of any, even the leaft Sin, which they have not taken care to blot out by Repentance, would neverthelefs go ftrait to Heaven?

*Q.* *Have you any other Text which the Fathers and Ecclefiaftical Writers interpret of Purgatory?*

*A.* Yes, 1 Cor. iii. *v.* 13, 14, 15. *Every man's work fhall be made manifeft. For the day fhall declare it, becaufe it fhall be revealed by fire. And the fire fhall try every man's work, of what fort it is. If any man's work abide which he hath built thereupon* [that is, upon the Foundation, which is *Jefus Chrift, v.* 11.] *he fhall receive a reward. If any man's work fhall be burnt, he fhall fuffer lofs:* BUT HE HIMSELF SHALL BE SAVED, YET SO AS BY FIRE. From which Text it appears, that fuch as both in their Faith, and in the Practice of their Lives, have ftuck to the Foundation, which is *Jefus Chrift,* fo as not to forfeit his Grace by mortal Sin; tho' they have otherwife been guilty of great Imperfections, by building *Wood, Hay,* and *Stubble,* (*v.* 12.) upon this Foundation; it appears, I fay, that fuch as thefe, according to the Apoftle, muft pafs thro' a fiery Trial, at the Time that *every man's work fhall be made manifeft*;

*fest* ; which is not till the next Life ; and that they fhall be *faved* indeed, *yet fo as by fire*, that is, by paffing firft thro' Purgatory.

2*dly*, Matt. v. *v.* 25, 26. *Agree with thine adverfary quickly, whilft thou art in the way with him: Left at any time the adverfary deliver thee to the judge, and the judge deliver thee to the officer, and thou be caft into prifon Verily, I fay unto thee, thou fhalt by no means come out thence till thou haft paid the uttermoft farthing.* Which Text St. *Cyprian*, one of the moft antient Fathers, underftands of the Prifon of Purgatory, *Epift.* 52. *ad Antonianum.*

3*dly*, Matt. xii. *v.* 32. *Whofoever fpeaketh againft the Holy Ghoft, it fhall not be forgiven him, neither in this world, neither in the world to come.* Which laft Words plainly imply, that fome Sins which are not forgiven in this World may be forgiven in the World to come : Otherwife, why fhould our Saviour make any Mention of Forgivenefs in the World to come ? Now if there may be Forgivenefs of Sins in the World to come, there muft be a Purgatory; for in Hell there is no Forgivenefs, and in Heaven no Sin.

Befides, a middle Place is alfo imply'd, 1 *Pet.* iii. *v.* 18, 19, 20. where *Chrift* is faid by his Spirit to have gone and *preach'd to the fpirits in prifon which fome time were difobedient*, &c. Which Prifon could be no other than Purgatory : For as to the Spirits that were in the Prifon of Hell, *Chrift* certainly did not go to preach to them.

Q. *How do you ground the Belief of Purgatory upon Tradition ?*

*A.* Becaufe both the *Jewifh* Church, long before our Saviour's Coming, and the *Chriftian* Church, from the very Beginning, in all Ages and all Nations, have offer'd Prayers and Sacrifice for the Repofe and Relief of the Faithful departed : As appears in regard to the *Jews* from 2 *Maccab.* xii. where this Practice

is

is approved of, which Books of *Maccabees*, the Church, fays St. *Augustin*, *L. 18. de Civ. Dei, c. 36*, accounts canonical, tho' the *Jews* do not. And in regard to the *Christian* Church, the fame is evident from all the Fathers, and the moft ancient Liturgies. Now fuch Prayers as thefe evidently imply the Belief of a Purgatory: For Souls in Heaven ftand in no Need of our Prayers, and thofe in Hell cannot be bettered by them.

Q. *How do you ground the Belief of Purgatory upon Reafon?*

*A.* Becaufe Reafon clearly teaches thofe two Things: 1ft, That all and every Sin, how fmall foever, deferves Punifhment. 2dly, That fome Sins are fo fmall, either through the Levity of the Matter, or for want of full Deliberation in the Action, as not to deferve eternal Punifhment. From whence it is plain, that befides the Place of eternal Punifhment, which we call Hell, there muft be alfo a Place of temporal Punifhment for fuch as die in little Sins, and this we call Purgatory.

✿✿✿✿✿✿✿✿✿✿✿✿✿✿✿✿✿✿✿✿✿✿✿

# CHAP. VIII.

## Of the Veneration and Invocation of Saints.

Q. *WHAT is the* Catholick *Doctrine touching the Veneration and Invocation of Saints?*

*A.* We are taught, 1ft, That there is an Honour and Veneration due to the Angels and Saints. 2dly, That they offer up Prayers to God for us. 3dly, That it is good and profitable to invoke them, that is, to have recourfe to their Interceffion and Prayers. 4thly, That their Relicks are to be had in Veneration.

SECT. 1. *Of the Veneration of the Angels and Saints.*

Q. *How do you prove that there is an Honour and Veneration due to the Angels and Saints?*

*A.* Becaufe they are God's Angels and Saints: That is to fay, moft faithful Servants, Courtiers, Friends, and Favourites of the King of Kings: Who, having highly honoured him, are now highly honoured by him, as he has promifed, 1 *Sam.* ii. *v.* 30. *Them that honour me I will honour.*

2*dly*, Becaufe they have received from their Lord moft eminent and fupernatural Gifts of *Grace* and *Glory*, which make them truly worthy of our Honour and Veneration, and therefore we give it them as their Due, according to that of the Apoftle, *Rom.* xiii. *v.* 7. *Honour to whom honour is due.*

3*dly*, Becaufe the Angels of God are our Guardians, Tutors, and Governors; as appears from many Texts of Scripture, Pf. xci. *v.* 11, 12. *He fhall give his angels charge over thee, to keep thee in all thy ways: they fhall bear thee up in their hands, left thou dafh thy foot againft a ftone.* Matt. xviii. *v.* 10. *Take heed that ye defpife not one of thefe little ones; for I fay unto you, that in heaven their angels do always behold the face of my father that is in heaven.* Heb. i. *v.* 14. *Are they not all miniftring fpirits, fent forth to minifter for them who fhall be heirs of falvation.* 'Tis therefore evidently the Will of God, that we fhould have a religious Veneration for thefe heavenly Guardians. Exodus xxii. *v.* 20, 21. *Behold I fend an angel before thee to keep thee in the way, and to bring thee into the place which I have prepared: beware of him, and obey his voice, provoke him not, for my name is in him.*

4*thly*, Becaufe God has promifed to his Saints a Power over all Nations, Rev. ii. *v.* 26, 27. *He that*

*that overcometh and keepeth my words unto the end, to him will I give power over the nations, and he shall rule them with a rod of iron---even as I received of my Father.* Rev. v. *v.* 10. *Thou hast made us unto our God kings and priests, and we shall reign on the earth.* Therefore all Nations ought to honour the Saints, as having received from God this kingly Power over them.

5*thly,* Becaufe we have Inftances in Scripture of Honour and Veneration paid to the Angels by the Servants of God: See *Joshua* v. *v.* 14, 15.

6*thly,* Becaufe the Church in all Ages has paid this Honour and Veneration to the Saints, by erecting Churches, and keeping Holidays in their Memory: A Practice which the *English* Proteftants have alfo retained.

Q. *Do you then worship the Angels and Saints as God, or give them the Honour that belongs to God alone?*

*A.* No, God forbid: For this would be a high Treafon againft his divine Majefty.

Q. *What is the Difference between the Honour which you give to God, and that which you give to the Saints?*

*A.* There is no Comparifon between the one and the other. We honour God with a fovereign Honour, as the fupreme Lord and Creator of all Things, as our firft Beginning and our laft End: We believe *in him alone*; we hope in him alone; we love him above all Things. To him alone we pay our Homage of divine Adoration, Praife, and Sacrifice: But as for the Saints and Angels, we only reverence them with an inferior Honour, *as belonging to him, for his Sake,* and *upon Account of the Gifts which they have received from him.*

Q. *Do you not give a particular Honour to the Virgin* Mary?

*A.* Yes, we do, by reafon of her eminent Dignity of *Mother of God,* for which *all generations shall call*

D 2 *her*

*her bleſſed,* Luke i. *v.* 48.   As alſo by reaſon of that Fulneſs of Grace which ſhe enjoyed in t··is Life, and the ſublime Degree of Glory to which ſhe is raiſed in Heaven.   But ſtill even this Honour which we give to her is infinitely inferior to that which we pay to God, to whom ſhe is indebted for all her Dignity, Grace, and Glory.

SECT. 2. *That the Saints and Angels pray to God for us.*

Q. *How do you prove this?*

*A.* 1*ſt,* From *Zechariah* i. *v.* 12. where the Prophet heard an Angel praying for *Jeruſalem* and the Cities of *Judah, The Angel of the Lord anſwered and ſaid, O Lord of Hoſts, how long wilt thou not have mercy on Jeruſalem and on the cities of Judah, againſt which thou haſt had indignation theſe threeſcore and ten years?*

2*dly,* From *Revel.* v. *v.* 8. *The four and twenty elders fell down before the Lamb, having every one of them harps and golden vials full of odours, which are the prayers of ſaints.*   And *Rev.* viii. *v.* 4. *The ſmoke of the incenſe, with the prayers of the ſaints, aſcended up before God out of t·e angel's hand.*   From which Texts it is evident, that both the Saints and Angels offer up to God the Prayers of the Saints, that is, of the Faithful upon Earth.

3*dly,* Becauſe we profeſs in the Creed *the Communion of Saints;* and St. *Paul, Heb.* xii. *v.* 22, 23, 24. ſpeaking to the Children of the Church of *Chriſt,* tells them that they have a Fellowſhip with the Saints in Heaven ; *You are come unto mount Sion, and unto the city of the living God, the heavenly Jeruſalem, and to an innumerable company of angels, to the general aſſembly and church of the firſt born which are written in heaven, and to the ſpirits of juſt men made perfect,* and to *Jeſus* the *Mediator,* &c.   Therefore the Children of the Church of *Chriſt* upon Earth

are

are Fellow-members with the Saints in Heaven of the same Body, under the under Head, which is *Christ Jesus.* Hence the same Apostle, *Galat.* iv. *v.* 26. calls the heavenly *Jerusalem our Mother* ; and *Ephes.* ii. *v.* 19. tells us, that we are *fellow citizens with the saints.* Therefore the Saints in Heaven have a Care and Solicitude for us, as being Members of the same Body, it being the Property of the Members of the same Body to be solicitous for one another, *1 Cor.* xii. *v.* 25, 26. Consequently the Saints in Heaven pray for us.

4*thly,* Because according to the Doctrine of the Apostle, *1 Cor.* xiii. *v.* 8 it is the Property of the Virtue of Charity not to be lost in Heaven, as Faith and Hope are their lost ; *Charity,* saith St. *Paul, never faileth.* On the contrary, this heavenly Virtue is perfected in Heaven, where, by seeing God Face to Face, the Soul is inflamed with a most ardent Love for God, and for his Sake loves exceedingly his Children, her Brethren here below : How then can the Saints in Heaven, having so perfect a Charity for us, not pray for us, since the very first Thing that Charity prompts a Person to do, is to seek to succour and assist those whom he loves?

5*thly,* Because we find, *Luke* xvi. *v.* 27, 28. the rich Glutton in Hell petitioning in Favour of his five Brethren here upon Earth : How much more are we to believe, that the Saints in Heaven interceed for their Brethren here?

6*thly,* Because, *Revel.* vi. *v.* 10. the Souls of the Martyrs pray for Justice against their Persecutors, who had put them to Death : How much more do they pray for Mercy for the faithful Children of the Church?

7*thly,* In fine. Because our Lord, *Luke* xvi. *v.* 9. tells us, *Make to yourselves friends of the mammon of unrighteousness ; that when ye fail, they may receive you into everlasting habitations.* Where he gives us to understand, that the Servants of God, whom we

have

have help'd by our Alms, after they themfelve have got to Heaven, help and affift us to enter into that everlafting Kingdom.

### SECT. 3. *Of the Invocation of Saints.*

Q. *What do you mean by the Invocation of Saints?*

*A.* I mean fuch Petitions or Requefts as are made to defire their Prayers and Interceffions for us.

Q. *Do Catholicks pray to Saints?*

*A.* If by *praying to Saints* you mean addreffing ourfelves to them as to the Authors or Difpofers of Grace and Glory, or in fuch Manner as to fuppofe that they have any Power to help us, independently of God's good Will and Pleafure, we do not *pray to them,* but condemn all fuch Addreffes as fuperftitious and impious. But if, by *praying to Saints,* you mean no more than defiring them to pray to God for us, in this Senfe we hold it both good and profitable to *pray to the Saints.*

Q. *How do you prove that it is good and profitable to defire the Saints and Angels in Heaven to pray to God for us?*

*A.* Becaufe it is good and profitable to defire the Servants of God here upon Earth to pray for us: *For the prayer of a righteous man availeth much,* *James* v. *v.* 16. *Mofes* by his Prayers obtained Mercy for the Children of *Ifrael, Exod.* xxxii. *v.* 11, 14. And *Samuel* by his Prayers defeated the *Philiftines,* 1 *Samuel* vii. *v.* 8, 9, 10. Hence St. *Paul,* in almoft all his Epiftles, defires the Faithful to pray for him, *Rom.* xv. *v.* 30. *Eph.* vi *v.* 18, 19. 1 *Theff.* v. *v.* 25. *Heb.* xiii. *v.* 13. And God himfelf, *Job* xliii. *v.* 8. commanded *Eliphaz* and his two Friends to go to *Job,* that *Job* fhould pray for them, promifing to accept of his Prayers. Now if it be acceptable to God, and good and profitable to ourfelves, to feek the Prayers and Interceffion of God's Servants here on Earth; muft it not be much more fo

to

to feek the Prayers and Interceffion of the Saints in Heaven; fince both their Charity for us, and their Credit and Intereft with God, is much greater now than when they were here upon Earth?

Q *But does it not argue a Want of Confidence in the infinite Goodnefs of God, and the fuperabounding Merits of* Jefus Chrift *our Redeemer, to addrefs ourfelves to the Saints for their Prayers and Interceffion?*

*A.* No more than to addrefs ourfelves to our Brethren here below, as Proteftants do when they defire the Prayers of the Congregaiton; fince we defire no more of the Saints than what we defire of our Brethren here below, *viz.* that they would pray for us, and with us, to the Infinite Goodnefs of God, who is both our Father and their Father, our Lord and their Lord, by the Merits of his Son *Jefus Chrift,* who is both our Mediator and their Mediator. For tho' the Goodnefs of God and the Merits of *Chrift* be infinite, yet as this is not to exempt us from frequent Prayer for ourfelves, fo much recommended in Scripture, fo 'tis no Reafon for our being backward in feeking the Prayers of others, whether in Heaven or Earth, that fo God may have the Honour, and we the Benefit, of fo many more Prayers.

Q. *But is there no Danger, by acting thus, of giving to the Saints the Honour which belongs to God alone?*

*A.* No; 'tis evident, that to defire the Prayers and Interceffion of the Saints is by no means giving them an Honour which belongs to God alone: So far from it, that it would even be a Blafphemy to beg of God to *pray for us;* becaufe whofoever defires any one to *pray for him* for the obtaining of a Grace or Bleffing, fuppofes the Perfon to whom he thus addreffes himfelf to be inferior and dependent of fome other by whom this Grace or Bleffing is to be beftowed.

Q. *Have you any Reafon to think that the Saints and Angel have any Knowledge of your Addreffes or Petitions made to them?*

*A.* Yes,

*A.* Yes, we have. 1*ſt*, Becauſe our Lord aſſures us, *Luke* xv. *v.* 10. That *there is joy in the preſence of the angels of God, over one ſinner that repenteth.* For if they rejoice at our Repentance, conſequently they have a Knowledge of our Repentance; and if they have a Knowledge of our Repentance, what Reaſon can we have to doubt of their knowing our Petitions alſo? And what is here ſaid of the Angels is alſo to be underſtood of the Saints, of whom our Lord tells us, *Luke* xx. *v.* 36. that *they are equal unto the angels.*

2*dly*, Becauſe the Angels of God, who, as we have already ſeen, are our *Guardians*, are always amongſt us, and therefore cannot be ignorant of our Requeſts; eſpecially ſince, as we have alſo ſeen from *Rev.* v. *v.* 8. and viii. *v.* 4. both Angels and Saints offer up our Prayers before the Throne of God, and therefore muſt needs know them.

3*dly*, Becauſe it appears from *Rev.* xi. *v.* 15. and *Rev.* xix. *v.* 1 and 2. that the Inhabitants of Heaven know what paſſeth upon Earth. Hence St. *Paul*, 1 *Cor.* iv. *v.* 9. ſpeaking of himſelf and his Fellow-Apoſtles, ſaith, *We are made a ſpectacle unto the world, and to angels, and to men.*

4*thly*, We cannot ſuppoſe that the Saints and Angels, who enjoy the Light of Glory, can be ignorant of ſuch Things as the Prophets and Servants of God in this World have often known by the Light of Grace, and even the very Devils by the Light of Nature alone: Since the Light of Glory is ſo much more perfect than the Light of Grace or Nature, according to the Apoſtle, 1 *Cor.* xiii. 12. *For now we ſee through a glaſs darkly; but then face to face: now I know in part; but then ſhall I know even as alſo I am known:* That is, by a moſt perfect Knowledge. Hence, 1 *John* iii. *v.* 2. it is written, *We ſhall be like him* (God) *for we ſhall ſee him as he is.* Now it is certain, that the Servants of God in this World, by a ſpecial Light of Grace, have often known

Things

Things that pafs'd at a great Diftance: As *Elisha*, 2 *Kings* v. knew what pafs'd between *Naaman* and his Servant *Gehazi*; and 2 *Kings* vi. what was done by the King of *Syria* in his private Chamber. 'Tis alſo certain, that the Devils, by the mere Light of Nature, know what paffes amongſt us, as appears by the Correfpondence they hold with Magicians, and by their being our Accuſers, *Rev.* xii. *v.* 10. Therefore we cannot reaſonably queftion, but that the Saints in Heaven know the Petitions which we addreſs unto them.

5*thly*, In fine, becauſe it is weak Reaſoning to argue from our corporal Hearing (the Object of which being *Sound*, that is, a Motion or Undulation of the Air, cannot reach beyond a certain Diftance) to the Hearing of Spirits, which is independent on Sound, and confequently independent of Diftance: Tho' the Manner of it be hard enough to explicate to thoſe who know no other Hearing but that of the corporal Ear.

Q. *Have you any other Warrant in Scripture for the Invocation of Angels and Saints?*

*A.* Yes; we have the Example of God's beſt Servants. Thus *Jacob*, Gen. xlviii. *v.* 15, 16. begs the Bleffing of his Angel Guardian for his two Grandſons, *Ephraim* and *Manaffeh*. *God, before whom my father Abraham and Iſaac did walk, the God which fed me all my life long until this day, the angel which redeemed me from all evil, bleſs the lads.* The ſame *Jacob*, Hofea xii. *v.* 4. *wept and made ſupplication to an angel.* And St. *John*, Rev. i. *v.* 4. writing to the ſeven Churches of *Aſia*, petitions for the Interceffion of the ſeven chief Angels in their Favour. *Grace be unto you, and peace from him, which is, and which was, and which is to come, and from the ſeven ſpirits which are before his throne.*

### SECT. 4. *Of Relicks.*

Q. *What do you mean by* Relicks?

*A.* The

*A.* The Bodies or Bones of Saints; or any Thing elfe that belong'd to them.

*Q. What Grounds have you for paying a Veneration to the Relicks of the Saints?*

*A.* Befides the ancient Tradition and Practice of the firft Ages, attefted by the beft Monuments of Antiquity, we have been warranted to do fo by many illuftrious Miracles done at the Tombs and by the Relicks of the Saints (fee St. *Auguftine*, L. 22. *Of the City of God*, cap. 8.) Which God, who is Truth and Sanctity itfelf, would never have effected, if this Honour paid to the precious Remnants of his Servants were not agreeable to him.

*Q. Have you any Inftances in Scripture of Miracles done by Relicks?*

*A.* Yes, we read, 2 *Kings* xiii. *v.* 21. of a dead Man rais'd to Life by the Bones of the Prophet *Elifha:* And *Acts* xix. *v.* 12. *From the body of Paul were brought unto the fick handkerchiefs or aprons, and the difeafes departed from them, and the evil fpirits went out of them.*

✤✤✤✤✤✤✤✤✤✤✤✤✤✤✤✤✤✤✤✤

## CHAP IX.

### *Of Images.*

*Q.* WH A T *is your Doctrine as to Images?*

*A.* We hold that the Images or Pictures of *Chrift*, of his bleffed Mother, ever Virgin, and of other Saints, are to be had and retain'd; and that due Honour and Veneration is to be given them.

*Q. Do you not worfhip Images?*

*A.* No, by no means, if by *Worfhip* you mean *divine Honour:* For this we don't give to the higheft Angel or Saint, no, nor even to the Virgin *Mary*, much lefs to Images.

*Q. Do you not pray to Images?*

*A.* No,

*A.* No, we don't: Becaufe as both our Catechifm and common Senfe teaches us, *They can neither fee, nor hear, nor help us.* Doway Catechifm.

Q. *Why then do you pray before an Image or Crucifix?*

*A.* Becaufe the Sight of a good Picture or Image, for Example, of *Chrift* upon the Crofs, helps to enkindle Devotion in our Hearts towards him, that has loved us to that Excefs, as to lay down his Life for the Love of us.

Q *Are you not taught to put your Truft and Confidence in Images, as the Heathens did in their Idols: as if there were a certain Virtue, Power or Divinity refiding in them?*

*A.* No, we are expreffly taught the contrary by the Counfel of *Trent,* Seffion 25.

Q. *How do you prove, that it is lawful to make or keep the Images of* Chrift *and his Saints?*

*A.* Becaufe God himfelf commanded *Mofes,* Exod. xxv. *v.* 18, 19, 20, 21. to make two Cherubims of beaten Gold, and place them at the two Ends of the Mercy-feat, over the Ark of the Covenant in the very Sanctuary. *And there,* fays he, *v.* 22. *will I meet with thee, and I will commune with thee from above the mercy-feat, from between the two Cherubims which are upon the ark of the teftimony, of all things which I will give thee in commandment unto the children of Ijrael.* God alfo commanded, *Numb.* xxi. *v.* 8, 9. a Serpent of Brafs to be made, for the healing of thofe who were bit by the fiery Serpents: Which Serpent was an Emblem of *Chrift,* John iii. *v.* 14, 15.

Q. *But is it not forbidden,* Exod xx. *v.* 4. to make the Likenefs of any thing in Heaven above, or in the Earth beneath, or in the Waters under the Earth?

*A.* It is forbidden *to make to ourfelves* any fuch Image or Likenefs; that is to fay, to make it our God, or put our Truft in it, and give it the Honour which belongs to God: Which is explain'd by the following

ing

ing Words, *Thou shalt not bow down thyself to them,* (that is, *thou shalt not adore them,* for so both the *Septuagint* and *Vulgate* tranflate it) *nor ferve them.* Otherwife, if all Likeneffes were forbid by this Commandment, we fhould be obliged to fling down our Sign-pofts, and deface the King's Coin.

Q. *What Kind of Honour do* Catholicks *give to the Images of* Chrift *and his Saints?*

*A.* A *relative Honour.*

Q. *What do you mean by a* relative Honour?

*A.* By a *relative Honour,* I mean an Honour which is given to a Thing, not for any intrinfick Excellence or Dignity in the Thing itfelf, but barely for the Relation it has to fomething elfe; as when the Courtiers bow to the Chair of State, or *Chriftians* to the Name of *Jefus,* which is an Image of Remembrance of our Saviour to the Ear, as a Crucifix is to the Eye.

Q. *Have you any Inftances of this relative Honour allow'd by* Proteftants?

*A.* Yes; in the Honour they give to the Name of *Jefus,* to their Churches, to the Altar, to the Bible, to the Symbols of Bread and Wine in the Sacrament. Such alfo was the Honour which the *Jews* gave to the Ark and Cherubims, and which *Mofes* and *Jofhua* gave to the Land on which they ftood, as being *holy ground,* Exod. iii. *v.* 5. *Jofh.* v. *v.* 15, &c.

Q. *How do you prove that there is a* relative Honour *due to the Images or Pictures of* Chrift *and his Saints?*

*A.* From the Dictates of common Senfe and Reafon, as well as of Piety and Religion, which teach us to exprefs our Love and Efteem for the Perfons whom we honour, by fetting a Value upon all Things that belong to them, or have any Relation to them: Thus a loyal Subject, a dutiful Child, a loving Friend, value the Pictures of their King, Father or Friend; and thofe who make no Scruple of abufing the Image of *Chrift,* would feverely punifh the Man that would abufe the Image of his King.

Q. *Does*

Q. *Does your Church allow of Images of God the Father, or of the blessed Trinity?*

*A.* Our Profeſſion of Faith makes no Mention of ſuch Images as theſe: Yet we don't think them unlawful, provided that they be not underſtood to bear any Likeneſs or Reſemblance of the Divinity, which cannot be expreſs'd in Colours, or repreſented by any human Workmanſhip. For as *Proteſtants* make no Difficulty of painting the Holy Ghoſt under the Figure of a Dove, becauſe he appear'd ſo when *Chriſt* was baptiz'd, *Mat.* ii. *v* 16. ſo we make no Difficulty of painting God the Father under the Figure of a Venerable Old Man, becauſe he appear'd in that Manner to the Prophet *Daniel,* chap. vii. *v.* 9.

❖❖❖❖❖❖❖❖❖❖❖❖❖❖❖❖❖❖❖❖❖

# CHAP. X.

## *Of Indulgences.*

Q. *W*HAT *do you mean by* Indulgences?

*A.* Not Leave to commit Sin, nor Pardon for Sins to come: But only a Releaſing, by the Power of the Keys committed to the Church, the Debt of temporal Puniſhment, which may remain due upon Account of our Sins, after the Sins themſelves, as to the Guilt and eternal Puniſhment, have been already remitted by Repentance and Confeſſion.

Q. *Can you prove from Scripture, that there is a Puniſhment often due upon Account of our Sins, after the Sins themſelves have been remitted?*

*A.* Yes, this evidently appears in the Caſe of King *David*; 2 *Sam.* 12. where, altho' the Prophet *Nathan,* upon his Repentance, tells him, *v.* 13. *The Lord hath put away thy ſin,* yet he denounces unto him many terrible Puniſhments, *v.* 10, 11, 12, 14. which ſhould be inflicted by reaſon of this Sin; which accordingly afterwards enſued.

Q. *What is the Faith of your Church touching Indulgences?*  E  *A.* 'Tis

*A.* 'Tis compris'd in thefe Words of our Profeffion of Faith : *I affirm that the Power of Indulgences was left by Chrift in the Church, and that the Ufe of them is moft wholefome to Chriftian People.*

*Q. Upon what Scripture do you ground this ?*

*A.* The Power of granting Indulgences was left by *Chrift* to the Church ; *Matt.* xvi. *v.* 19. *I will give unto thee the keys of the kingdom of heaven : And whatfoever thou fhalt bind on earth, fhall be bound in Heaven : And whatfoever thou fhalt loofe on earth, fhall be loos'd in Heaven.* And we have an Inftance in Scripture of St. *Paul's* granting an Indulgence to the *Corinthian* whom he had put under Penance for Inceft : 2 *Cor.* ii. *v.* 10. *To whom ye forgive any thing* (he fpeaks of the Inceftous Sinner whom he had defired them now to receive) *I forgive alfo : For if I forgave any thing, to whom I forgave it, for your fakes forgave I it in the Perfon of* Chrift : That is, by the Power and Authority receiv'd from him.

❖❖❖❖❖❖❖❖❖❖❖❖❖❖❖❖❖❖❖❖❖

# C H A P. XI.

*Of the Supremacy of St.* Peter *and his Succeffors.*

*Q. WHAT is the Catholick Doctrine as to the Pope's Supremacy ?*

*A.* It is comprifed in thefe two Articles ; 1. That St. *Peter* by divine Commiffion was Head of the Church under *Chrift.* 2. That the Pope, or Bifhop of *Rome,* as Succeffor to St. *Peter,* is at prefent Head of the Church, and *Chrift's* Vicar upon Earth.

*Q. How do you prove St.* Peter's *Supremacy ?*

*A. Firft,* From the very Name of *Peter* or *Cephas,* which fignifies *a Rock,* which Name our Lord, who does nothing without Reafon, gave to him, who before was call'd *Simon,* to fignify that he fhould be as *the Rock* or *Foundation* upon which he would build his Church. According to what he himfelf declared, *Mat.*

xvi.

xvi. *v.* 18. when he told him, *Thou art* Peter (that is, *a Rock*) *and upon* THIS ROCK *will I build my Church, and the Gates of Hell shall not prevail against it.*

2d'y, From the following Words, *Matt.* xvi. *v.* 19. *I will give unto thee the keys of the kingdom of heaven, and whatsoever thou shalt bind on earth, shall be bound in heaven: And whatsoever thou shalt loose on earth, shall be loos'd in heaven.* Where, under the Figure of *the keys of the kingdom of heaven,* our Lord ensureth to *Peter* the chief Authority in his Church: As when a King gives to one of his Officers the Keys of a City, he thereby declares that he makes him Governor of that City.

3dly, From *Luke* xxii. *v.* 31, 32. *The Lord said,* Simon, Simon, *behold Satan hath desired to have you, that he may sift you as wheat. But I have pray'd for thee, that thy faith fail not, and when thou art converted strengthen thy brethren.* In which Text our Lord not only declared his particular Concern for *Peter,* in praying for him, that his Faith might not fail; but also committed to him the Care of his Brethren the other Apostles, in charging him to confirm or strengthen them.

4thly, From *John* xxi. *v.* 15, &c. Jesus *saith to* Simon Peter, Simon *Son of* Jonas *lovest thou me more than these? He saith unto him, Yea, Lord, thou knowest that I love thee. He saith unto him,* FEED MY LAMBS: *He said to him again the second time,* Simon *Son of* Jonas *lovest thou me? He saith unto him, Yea, Lord, thou knowest that I love thee. He saith unto him,* FEED MY SHEEP. *He saith unto him, the third time,* Simon *Son of* Jonas *lovest thou me?* Peter *was griev'd because he said unto him the third time lovest thou me? And he said unto him, Lord, thou knowest all things, thou knowest that I love thee:* Jesus *saith unto him,* FEED MY SHEEP. In which Text our Lord in a most solemn Manner thrice committed to *Peter* the Care of his whole Flock, of

all

all his Sheep without Exception, that is, of his whole Church.

Q. *How do you prove that this Commiffion given to* Peter *defcends to the Pope or Bifhop of* Rome ?

*A.* Becaufe by the unanimous Confent of the Fathers, and the Tradition of the Church in all Ages, the Bifhops of *Rome* are the Succeffors of St. *Peter*, who tranflated his Chair from *Antioch* to *Rome*, and died Bifhop of *Rome.* Hence the See of *Rome* in all Ages is call'd *The See of* Peter, *the Chair of* Peter, and abfolutely the *See Apoftolick :* And in that Quality has from the Beginning exercis'd Jurifdiction over all other Churches, as appears from the beft Records of antient Church-Hiftory.

Befides, fuppofing the Supremacy of St. *Peter*, which we have proved above from plain Scripture; it muft confequently be allowed that this Supremacy which *Chrift* eftablifhed for the better Government of his Church, and maintaining of Unity, was not to die with *Peter*, no more than the Church, which he promis'd fhould ftand for ever. For how can any *Chriftian* imagine, that *Chrift* fhould appoint a Head for the Government of his Church, and maintaining of Unity during the Apoftles Time ; and defign another kind of Government for fucceeding Ages, when there was like to be fo much more need of a Head. Therefore we muft grant that St. *Peter*'s Supremacy was by Succeffion to defcend to fome body. Now I would willingly know who has half fo fair a Title to this Succeffion as the Bifhop of *Rome ?*

Q. *Why do you call the* Roman *Church* the Mother and Miftrefs of all Churches ?

*A.* Becaufe, as we have already feen, her Bifhop is St. *Peter*'s Succeffor, and *Chrift*'s Vicar upon Earth ; and confequently the Father and Paftor of all the Faithful : And therefore this Church, as being St. *Peter*'s See, is the Mother and Miftrefs of all Churches.

CON-

## CONCLUSION.

Q. *HAVE you any thing more to add in Confirmation of all thefe Tenets contain'd in your Profeffion of Faith?*

*A.* I fhall add no more than this, that having already proved in the firft Chapter, that the Church in Communion with *Rome* is the true and only Church of *Chrift*, and confequently her Councils and Paftors the Guides of divine Appointment, which *Chrift* has eftablifh'd to be our Conductors in the Way to a happy Eternity; it follows that we fhould without further Hefitation believe and profefs, what this Church and her Paftors believe and profefs; and condemn and reject, what they condemn and reject: Affuring ourfelves that by doing thus we fhall be fecure, fince we fhall follow thofe Guides which *Chrift* himfelf has appointed, whom he has commanded us to hear, and with whom he has promis'd to abide to the End of the World

Q. *Why do you in your Profeffion of Faith make a Declaration of receiving in particular the Doctrine of the Council of* Trent?

*A.* Becaufe this was the laft general Council, call'd in Oppofition to the new Doctrines of *Luther* and *Calvin:* And therefore we particularly declare our Affent to the Decrees of this Council, as being levell'd againft thofe Herefies which have been moft prevalent in thefe two laft Ages.

May the God of Unity, Peace and Truth, by his infinite Mercy, conduct all *Chriftians* to Unity, Peace and Truth. *Amen. Amen.*

## *An* APPENDIX.

IN which are briefly propos'd the Motives, or rational Inducements, to the *Catholick* Faith, which, according to Dr. *Jeremy Taylor*, a learned *Proteftant* Prelate (*Lib. of Proph. Sect.* 20. *p.* 249, 250.) *may*

*very*

*very eafily perfuade Perfons of much Reafon and more Piety to retain that which they know to have been the Religion of their Forefathers, and which had actual Poffeffion and Seizure of Men's Underftandings before the oppofite Profeffions had a Name*; *p.* 251.

1ft, *I confider,* fays he, *p.* 249, *that thofe Doctrines that have had long Continuance and Poffeffion in the Church, cannot eafily be fuppofed in the prefent Profeffors to be a Defign, fince they have receiv'd it from fo many Ages.*---*Long Prefcription is a Prejudice oftentimes fo infupportable, that it cannot with many Arguments be retrench'd, as relying upon thefe Grounds, that Truth is more ancient than Falfhood*; *that God would not for fo many Ages forfake his Church*; *and leave her in an Error*; *that whatfoever is New is not only Sufpicious but Falfe: Which are Suppofitions pious and plaufible enough.* We have proved them to be not only *pious and plaufible Suppofitions,* but the plain Doctrine of the Word of God; *Chap.* 1. *Sect.* 1. and 3. He adds for other Motives,

2. *The Beauty and Splendor of their Church*; *their pompous Services*; *the Statelinefs and Solemnity of the Hierarchy.*

3. *Their Name of* CATHOLICK, *which they fuppofe their own Due.* They have certainly Reafon to fuppofe fo, if the Poffeffion or Prefcription of 17 Ages can make it their Due. I am fure it his fix'd it fo ftrongly upon them, that even their Adverfaries cannot help giving it them on many Occafions.

4. *The Antiquity of many of their Doctrines.* He fhould have faid *All*; but this could not be expected from a *Proteftant.*

5. *The continual Succeffion of their Bifhops*; *their immediate Derivation from the Apoftles.*

6. *Their Title to fucceed St.* Peter; *the Suppofal and Pretence of his perfonal Prerogatives*; grounded upon plain Scripture, as we have feen *chap.* xi. and therefore no vain Pretence.

7. *The Multitude and Variety of People which are of their Perfuafion.*　　　　　　　　　8. *Ap-*

8. *Apparent Confent with Antiquity, in many Cere-monials which other Churches have rejected: And a pretended and fometimes an apparent Confent with fome elder Ages in many Matters Doctrinal.* Here he minces the Matter for fear of allowing too much; yet can-not diffemble, that venerable Antiquity is apparently on the *Catholick* Side.

9. *The great Confent of one. Part with another in that which moft of them affirm to be of Faith. The great Differences commenced among their Adverfaries.* Whofe firft Fathers and Teachers, from the very Be-ginning of their pretended Reformation, went quite different Ways, even to an utter Breach of Commu-nion, which never fince could be repaired.

10. *Their Happinefs of being Inftruments in convert-ing divers Nations.* Whereas none of the reformed Churches have ever yet converted one.

11. *The Piety and the Aufterity of their religious Or-ders of Men and Women. The fingle Life of their Priefts and Bifhops---The Severity of their Fafts and their exterior Obfervances.* All which the good na-tur'd Reformation has laid afide.

13. *The great Reputation of their firft Bifhops for Faith and Sanctity. The known Holinefs of fome of thofe Perfons, whofe Inftitutes the Religious Perfons pre-tend to imitate.*

13. *Their Miracles, true or falfe,* fays the Doctor: True, fay I, if any Faith may be given to the moft certain Records of all Nations.

14. *The Cafualties and Accidents that have hap-pened to their Adverfaries.* I fuppofe he means fuch as *Luther*'s fudden Death after a plentiful Supper; *Zuing-lius*'s falling in Battle, defending his reform'd Gofpel Sword in Hand; *Oecomlopadius*'s being found dead in his Bed, opprefs'd, as *Luther* will have it, ( *L. de Miff. private & unct. facred. T.* 7. Wit. *fol.* 230.) by the Devil ; *Calvin*'s dying of a ftrange Complication of Diftempers, confumed alive by Vermin, *&c.*

15. *The*

15. *The oblique Arts and indirect Proceedings of some of those who departed from them.* In manifeftly corrupting the Scripture, as the firft *Proteftants* did in all their Tranflations, to make it chime with their Errors; in quoting falfly the Fathers and Ecclefiaftical Writers; in perpetually mifreprefenting in their Sermons and Writings the *Catholick* Church and her Doctrine; a Fault from which the Doctor himfelf is not exempt &c.

I have pafs'd over fome other Things of lefs Weight, which he alledges in the fame Place, and fhall only defire the Reader to compare the Motives which, by the Conceffion of this Prelate, fo much efteemed by all *Proteftants,* may retain *Catholicks* at prefent in the Religion of their Forefathers, with thofe Motives which St. *Auguftin* alledg'd, 1300 Years ago, againft the Hereticks of his Time, and by which he declares himfelf to have been retain'd in the *Catholick* Church, *L. contra Epiftolam Fund. C. 4.* ' Not to fpeak, ' fays he, of that true Wifdom which you do not be-' lieve to be in the *Catholick* Church; there are ma-' ny other Things which moft juftly hold me in ' her Communion. 1. The *Agreement of People and* ' *Nations.* 2. Her *Authority* begun by *Miracles,* nou-' rifh'd by Hope, encreas'd by Charity, confirm'd by ' *Antiquity.* 3. A *Succeffion* of Prelates defcending ' from *Peter* the *Apoftle,* to whom *Chrift,* after his ' Refurrection, committed his Flock to the prefent ' Bifhop. *Laftly,* The very *Name* of *Catholick,* of ' which this Church alone has, not without Reafon, in ' fuch Manner kept the Poffeffion, that tho' all Here-' ticks defire to be call'd *Catholicks,* yet, if a Stranger ' afk them where the *Catholicks* go to Church, none ' of them all has the Face to point out his own Church ' or Meeting-Houfe.' Thefe were St. *Auguftin's* Motives for being a *Catholick,* and thefe are ours.

Befides, we cannot diffemble that there were many fhocking Circumftances in the whole Management of the pretended Reformation, which deter us from

em-

embracing it, whatever temporal Inconveniences we are forced to sustain by this Recusancy.

1. The first Reformer *Martin Luther* had nothing of extraordinary Edification in his Life and Conversation. On the contrary, all his Works declare him to have been a Man of an implacible Nature, rigidly self-willed, impatient of Contradiction, and rough and violent in his Declamations against all those, of what Quality soever, who diffented in the least from him. But what was the most scandalous in a pretended Restorer of the Purity of Religion, was his marrying a Nun, after the most solemn Vows by which both he and she had confecrated themselves to God in the State of perpetual Continency. In which he was imitated by a great Part of the first reformed Ministers.

2. He and his first Affociates were certainly Schifmaticks, becaufe they feparated themfelves from all Churches pure or impure, true or falfe, that were then upon Earth, and ftood alone upon their own Bottom. Therefore if there was any fuch Thing then in the World as *the true Church of* Chrift (as there muft always be if the Scripture and Creed be true) *Luther* and his Fellows feparating from all Churches muft have feparated from the true, and confequently muft have been Schifmaticks, *At firft*, fays *Luther*, in the Preface to his Works, *I was all alone.* Which is confirm'd by Dr. *Tillotfon*, Serm. 49. p. 588. and Mr. *Colier*, in his *Hiftorical Dictionary*, under *Martin Luther*, where he praifes his Magnanimity in having *oppofed himfelf alone to the whole Earth.*

3. It appears from his Book *de Mifj. Privata & Unct. Sacred. T 7.* Wit. *Fol.* 228, *&c.* that he learnt no fmall Part of his Reformation from the Father of Lies, in a nocturnal Conference, of which he there gives his Readers an Account.

4. Thofe that were the moft bufy in promoting the Reformation here at Home, were for the moft Part Men of moft wretched Characters, fuch as K. *Hen.*

*Hen.* VIII. and the leading Men in the Government during the Minory of *Edw.* VI. not to fpeak of the Miniftry of Q. *Elizabeth, the moft wicked,* fays a late *Proteftant* Hiftorian, *(Short View of* Eng. *Hift. p.* 273.) *that ever was known in any Reign.*

5. The Foundations of the Reformation of *England* were laid by manifold Sacrileges, in pulling down Monafteries and other Houfes confecrated to God, rifling and pillaging Churches, alienating Church Lands, &c. as may be feen in the Hiftory of the Reformation by Dr. *Heylin.*

6. The Reformation was every where introduc'd by Lay Authority, and for the moft Part in direct Oppofition to, and contempt of the Bifhops, the Church Guides of divine Appointment. A Proceeding fanifeftly irregular and unjuftifiable, that in Church Matters the leity, with a few of the inferior Clergy, and thofe under the Ecclefiaftical Cenfures, fhould take upon them to direct thofe whom *Chrift* appointed to be their Directors.

7. *England* herfelf, which glories moft in the Regularity of her Reformation, compared to the tumultuous Proceedings of Reformers abroad, owes her prefent Eftablifhment of the Church to the Lay Authority of Q. *Elizabeth* and her Parliament, in Oppofition to all the Bifhops then fitting (who were all but one difpleafed for their Non-Conformity) to the whole Convocation, and both the Univerfities; that is, in a Word, to the whole Clergy of the Kingdom; as appears from *Fuller,* L. 9. and Dr. *Heylin,* Hift. of the Ref. *p.* 285, 286.

8. Wherefoever the reform'd Gofpel was preach'd, it brought forth Seditions, Tumults, Rebellions, &c. as appears from all the Hiftories of thofe Times. Infomuch, that in *France* alone, the reform'd Gofpellers, befides innumerable other Outrages, are faid to have deftroy'd no lefs than twenty thoufand Churches. *Jerufalem* and *Babel,* p. 158. How little does fuch a Reformation refemble the firft Eftablifhment of the Church of *Chrift!*                    9. The

9. The Fruits of the Reformation were such as could not spring from a good Tree. 1. An innumerable Spawn of Heresies. 2. Endless Dissentions. 3. A perpetual Itch of Changing, and Inconstancy in their Doctrine. 4. *Atheism, Deism, Latitudinarianism,* and barefaced Impiety. In fine, a visible Change of Manners for the worse, as many of their own Writers freely acknowledge, and old *Erasmus* long ago objected to them, *Ep. ad Vultur.* where he difies them to shew him one who had been reclaimed from Vice by going over to their Religion; and he declares he never yet met with one who did not seem chang'd for the worse.

10. That Religion is the best to live in which is the safest to die in, and that in the Judgment of dying Men, who are not like to be biafs'd at that Time by Interest, Humour, or Passion. Now it is certain, that Thousands, who have lived *Protestants,* have desir'd to die *Catholicks,* and never yet one that had lived a *Catholick* desired to die a *Protestant*; therefore it must be safest for us to stay where we are.

11. That Religion is preferable to all others, the Doctrine and Preaching of which is, and always has been more forcible and efficacious in order to the taking off Men's Minds from the perishable Goods of this World, and fixing them wholly on the great Business of Eternity; but such is the Doctrine and Preaching of the *Catholick* Church, as appears from those Multitudes of holy Solitaries in our Church that have retir'd themselves from all the Advantages to which their Birth or Fortune entitled them, and abandon'd all earthly Hopes for the Love of Heaven. Whereas the Reformation has never yet produced any such Fruits.

12. There was a true saving Faith in the Days of our Forefathers before the pretended Reformation, by which great Numbers are certainly arrived at the happy Port of eternal Felicity. Our Histories are all full of Instances of Charity, Piety, and Devotion of Kings, Bishops, &c. of the old Religion. Therefore

fore it is safer to follow their Faith than venture our Souls in a new raised Communion.

13. All ancient Pretenders to Reformation, (*i. e.* all those that ever undertook to alter or amend the Church's Faith) were condemned by the ancient Church for *Hereticks*, and are acknowledg'd to have been such by *Protestants* themselves. Therefore there is just Reason to apprehend left *Protestants* walking in the same Path may be involved in the same Misfortune.

14. In fine, *Protestants*, to defend their Reformation, condemn'd at its first Appearance by the Church Guides of divine Appointment, are forc'd to have Recourse to a Rule of Faith, which, if allow'd of, would set all both ancient and modern *Hereticks* out of the Reach of Church Authority. They are forced to appeal to a Tribunal, at which it is not possible that any Sectary should ever be condemn'd. Such a Rule, such a Tribunal is the Scripture, interpreted, not by Authority of Church Guides, but by every one's private Judgment : For this in effect is making every one's private Judgment the supreme Judge both of the Scripture, and of all Controversies in Religion, and authorizing him to prefer his own Whimsies before the Judgment of the whole Church. Could it be consistent with the Wisdom and Providence of God to leave his Church without some more certain Means of deciding Controversies and maintaining Unity? No certainly.

### F I N I S.

❀❀❀❀❀❀❀❀❀❀❀❀❀❀❀❀❀❀❀❀❀❀❀❀

N. B. *That in the foregoing Sheets, in quoting the Scripture, we have follow'd the common* Protestant Bible, *for the Sake of a great Part of our Readers that may have been accustomed to it : Not designing thereby to declare our Approbation of that Version, much less to give it the Preference to our* Catholick, Rhemish, *and* Doway *Translations.*

www.ingramcontent.com/pod-product-compliance
Lightning Source LLC
Chambersburg PA
CBHW031748090426
42739CB00008B/927